HOLLI MET THE METAL GODS

PART I

RUDOLPH T. RAVE

HOLLI MET THE METAL GODS

PART I

This book is dedicated to

the most important rockstar in my life:

Cheers!

LEMMY KILMISTER (R.I.P)

1945-2015

Translation from the German editon

by Donald Campbell, Steve Pederson

Prologue

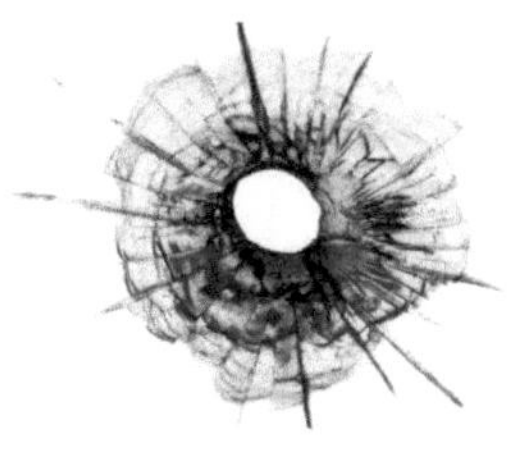

My name is Hollister Bluni. For my buddies I'm simply Holli. I worked as a photographer and editor for a few select metal-fanzines in the early 90's when Germany was still east and west—coming from the western side. It was always first row for me, struggling a lot. In order to breathe life into these small fanzines, we experienced a lot of things. Not all of them were positive, but the good experiences outweigh the bad ones.

In the here and now, after my career as annoying paparazzi and sleazy writer I need to write down some of those crazy stories. My psychiatrist said this would definitely help me. This would help my burnt soul finding peace at the end of this long and rocky road.

O.K., lets get serious: my psychiatrist as well as my funky sounding name is a mockery of my fantasy.
I only chose this name in order to be safe from the thousands of fans camping at my house, invading my privacy, trying get an autograph or whatever their fantasy is. I am definitely not the latest iPhone release, but then again—you never know! To make it short and sweet, my real name and my colleagues' names are of no interest for anybody. I hope you have a pleasant read during my voyage into the past and a reconnaissance with many, mostly still active, stars from the world of metal.

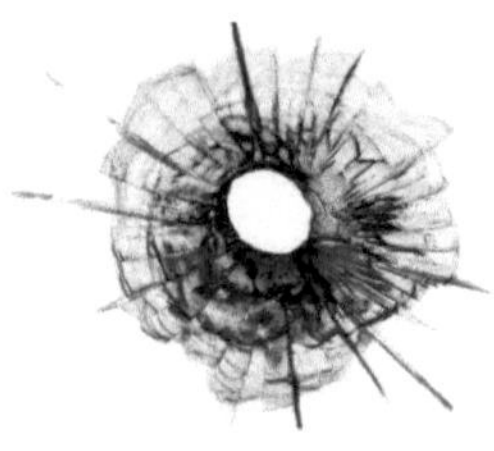

Papyrus Metallos

Far, far away, in a time before the emergence of the electronic spider, which spread her web across our globe, there were magazines printed on paper. These days, it seems that this certain way of circulating news is becoming more and more extinct. But at the end of the 70's and the beginning of the 80's—exactly this—was the most important, almost stand-alone source for us metal aficionados.

So, if I wanted to get news about those guys who were celebrating metallic shredder orgies, I was always keen on the latest news coming from that scene. Insatiable, as it is buried deep in human's nature, the thirst for more was always there, the same goes for me of course.

Since heavy metal was regarded more as an active form of revolution in the mainstream media such as tv or radio who both neglected this fine art of music—the only thing remaining were newspapers and propaganda from mouth to mouth. It may sound old-fashioned, but this strenuous gathering of information is considered by me as way more interesting than today's overload. These days you don't discover bands anymore, they get served on a daily base. You can't approach your buddy with amazing, ear-splitting, and violent metal-news anymore, he is already in the know thanks to big brother.

The big music-magazines from that time way back then only showed the polished-up versions of the industry in their releases. Something had to be done ASAP, so the resistance against the loud soup oozing from the outside could grow. Money for a radio-station? Nope. Money for your own tv-station? Nope again. Maybe money for your own publishing-company? Nope again...for the third time.

In many parts of the world, the first mags of the well-known Rock Hard magazine spawned out of a copy machine. And the only thing these guys were asking for, far away from the demands of the industry, was; SUPPORT THE UNDERGROUND.

The publishers main interest was to feature the band they really liked or were absolutely interested in. Created by fans for fans. Honest to the bone—the way it should be—and independent, as much as possible. As with anything which is really cool the community of metalheads was a vast growing one. The fan-mags, short form is fanzines, were increasing in size! Bigger companies got attracted by this underground movement and suddenly showed interest where neglect was a daily routine before. So was the independence in grave danger?
Yes, of course. Some mags made it this way, selling out a bit more and more, into the colorful world of high gloss magazines and huge print runs, don't take this too negative, by the way. Once you got cash flowing from the bigger companies, there is always that certain danger of dependency. It always was and shall remain a walk on the thin line between offering the readers a nice magazine or just plant a big brownie into the bowl and raise your finger towards the industry. The enthusiasm of the small, maybe not so significant magazines was unbroken though.

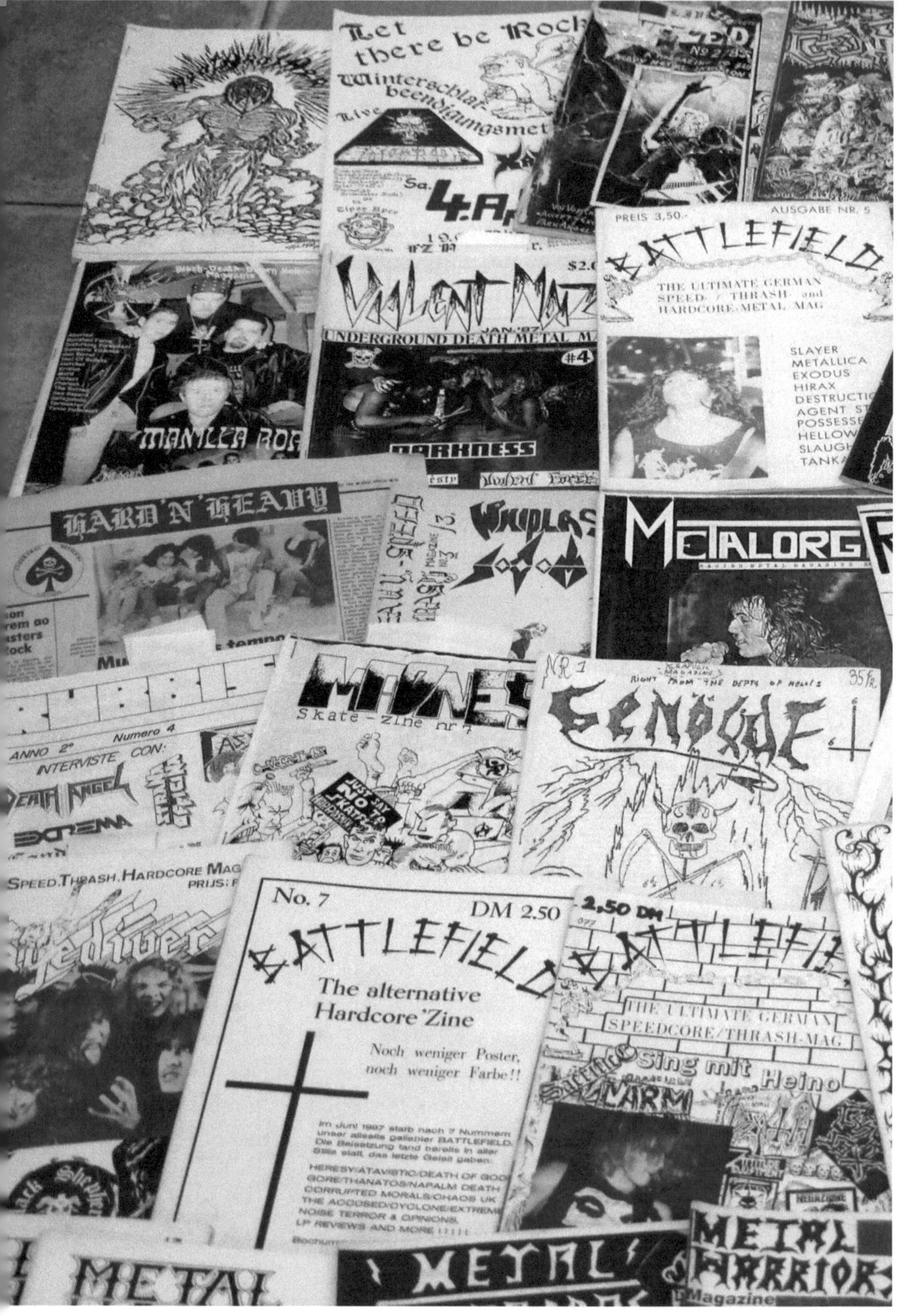

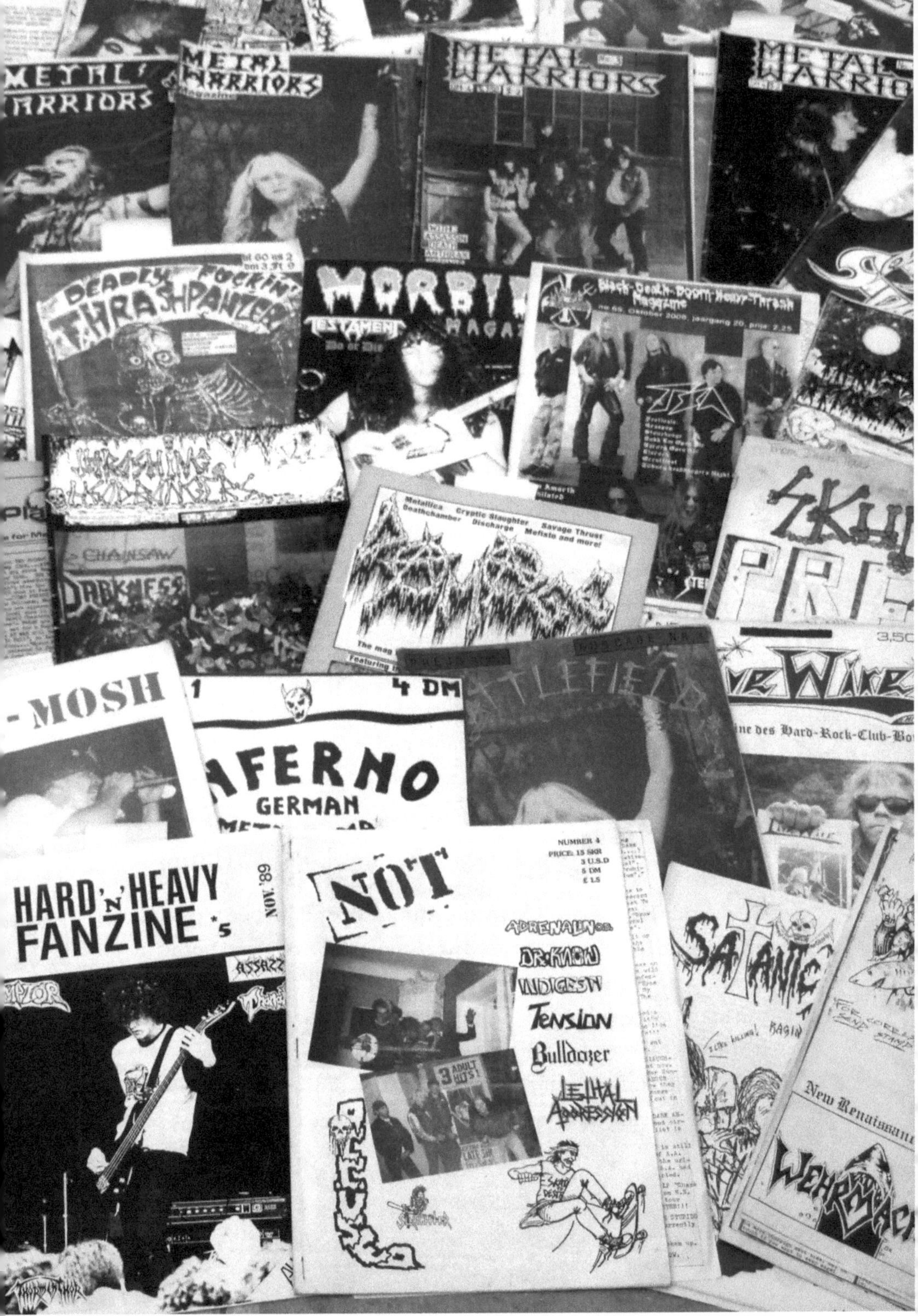

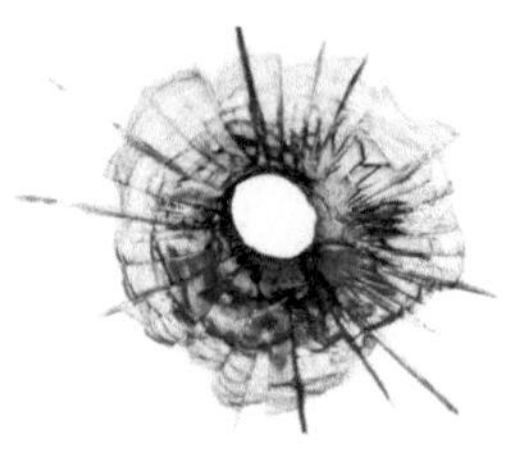

Nostalgica

The idea to invest your complete spare-time into your music and the fitting way of life was the first step. To create a fanzine for all your soul brothers content was in demand. O.K., easy job! Then you had to find a victim responsible for the appearance of the printed pages, without the help of a computer, it was the time of cut and paste (scissors and paper, sounds strange?). This is how it worked:

You grab a pencil, a sheet of paper and have a wastebasket at your side. Either you created a desired record-review or you listened to your tape-recordings to the voice of your interviewed rock star, desperately trying to interpret the babbling of the interviewed person. The very first Q&A games started when you went to your neighbor—band in the complex where all bands rehearsed, they were among the first victims to be promoted.

Criticizing records was an easy task, since everybody had tons of records at home. Once the initial text had been completed after quite a few attempts, the time was ripe for typing it all clean and mistake-free with an old typewriter, again: no mistakes here allowed! Otherwise the paper-basket peaked out from the flood of paper balls being thrown towards its gaping hole. After all this had been done, the old cut and paste game started. So the well-arranged text got cut into shape, several text blocks, the band-logos were mostly drawn by hand (at this time, scanners had not been invented yet) and a few pics. All this arranged neat and nicely and with the help of the newly invented glue stick, finally applied to a sheet of paper. When this strenuous task had been completed, say 15-20 times, so that this was really ready for print, the next honorable task ways the gathering of all the sheets and then the way to the local copy-shop. Everything else would have completely crashed the existing-or better said-non-existing budget which was available for doing a fanzine. It was more a labor of love than anything else.

Now it's time for some smartass-comments a la: "Why don't you get advertisers into the mag?"

Easier said than done. Doing something like 500 copies was absolutely uninteresting for record companies. Absolutely nobody cared about a fanzine—only the core-fans among themselves. When you lucked out you had your copy shop as advertising-partner, or maybe the local liquor store. But that's already the end of the story. Whatever, enough whining! Its all about doing it!!!!!!!!!!!!!!!!!!!!!!!!!

Way more important than the ugly business side were those things which made the fanzine what it should be in the end: interviews, reviews, concert critiques or the rant 'n' rave about local pubs—which were not too shy to feature metal as a daily dose for the visitors, even if they only did it once in a week. To make things smooth hand drawn illustrations and pics crowned the masterpiece. The publisher, chief-editor, editor, photographer, designer and slave of the typewriter was, as in all known cases, the same person. This person is called Sascha in my story.

I still remember the day when we first met. The Osterthrash-Festival 1990 in Konz near Trier. He was hustling around through the hall, busy looking guy.
He dwarfed my appearance with only 5' 3" in height. His hair already made it across the magic line where you know that he will never qualify as a trainee for a bank. There was this red leather jacket, which looked like something from an official and this set him apart from the crowd which was dressed in black, made him outstanding somehow. But underneath you could see the shimmer of a very cool shirt, it was FORBIDDEN! Anyway, the outfit doesn't really matter, metalhead is metalhead!!!!

We went all the way down from Northrhine-Westfalia, not only to see all those cool bands, most important was seeing Michael Hoffmann, who played with ASSASSIN for years and now joined SODOM, he was the lead-guitarist. Two of us knew him personally. So we spoke with Sascha, due to the fact that we both knew the same persons and he told us about his fanzine-work which sounded really interesting. He was loaded with work and looking for reliable dudes. Well, we were on the same page from the beginning, which lead into the consummation of a lot of beers. After some time we were trying to create word-games referring to the city we were in, the more we had, the stranger the result.

KONZentrate or KONZert were among the harmless

associations. With all the beer involved in this process, the main goal: search new co-worker for the mag, somehow got drowned to say so.

A few weeks later we met again by pure coincidence at a local pub, which is very famous for its metal-tradition, it's named PAPIDOUX and located in the center of our famous old town. So Sascha ended up telling me again what he is doing and I thought: "Man, this is cool", which led to the final question if I was interested in joining the mag and also being able to start working on things the next day.

This was the beginning of an extremely thrilling time for me.

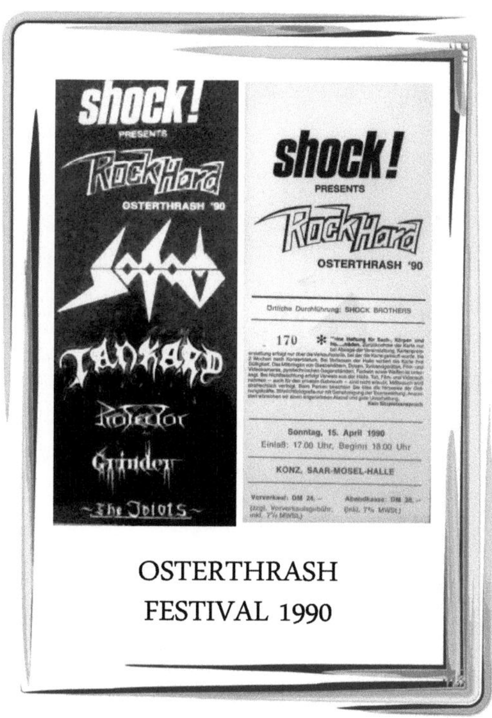

OSTERTHRASH
FESTIVAL 1990

My first time

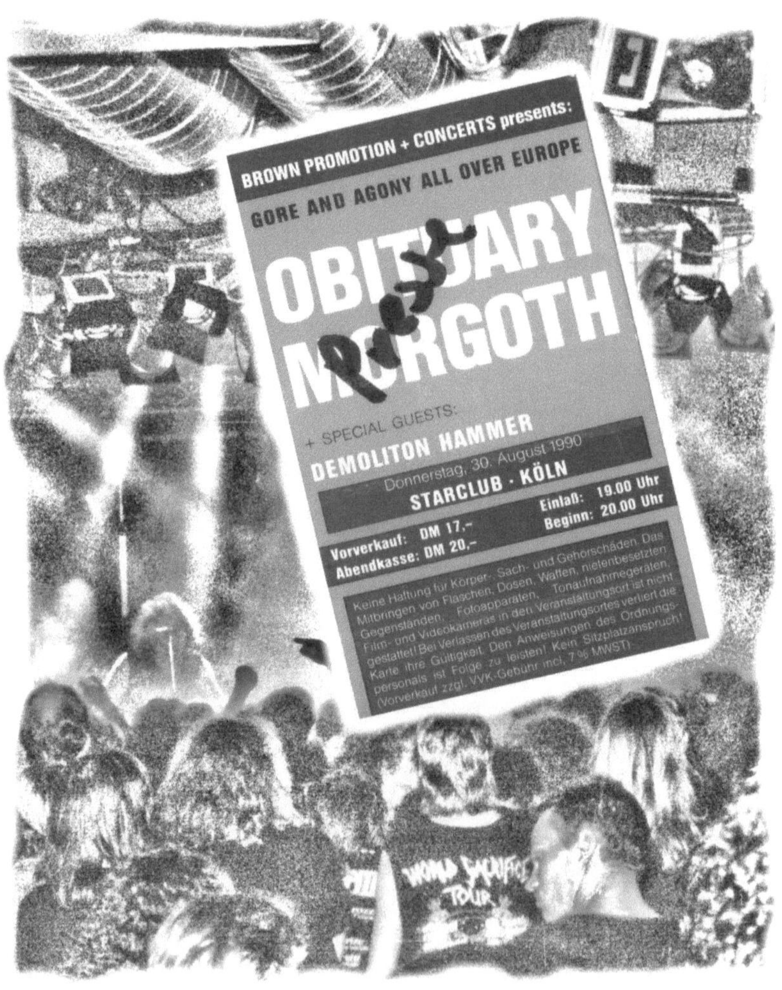

The next day Sascha called me at home and said:"It's on!!!, our names are on the list. We go to Cologne, to the Star Club. Make sure you got your camera with you."
Due to all the atmospheric interruptions I was still suffering from the day before I just said "ok, I'm game", completely unaware of anything at all. When I got clearer in my head the first question which arose was the location of the Star Club. I always thought it was located in Hamburg, it got famous when the BEATLES played there in the 60's. Wahtever...who the fuck cares?...on the trip to Cologne Sascha briefed me regarding the whereabouts and who was supposed to rock the place.

MORGOTH, OBITUARY and DEMOLITION HAMMER

OMG yeahhhh come on woweeeeeeeeeeeeeeeeee. The line-up was complete awesomeness for me, only Demolition Hammer was completely unknown for me, the rest was a total pleasure for my ears.
"If everything goes ok and they didn't tell me shit we are on the guest-list as press with extra tickets for taking pictures aaaand we are supposed to do an interview ."
Way cool....that was my first thought. You see some really cool bands, you are allowed to take a few pics and then you can talk with your rock-stars. Getting free entry was almost unimportant with all those benefits in mind.

The very first stop for each roadtrip to a concert was the next gas-station in the city to be visited. You ask the owner for directions and move on.in case of failure, which was quite often the case, the next gas-station was the solution...sometimes...yes...these were the good old days.

Having arrived at the show Sascha made it to the ticket-counter and volia he rev´ceived the press-tix without any stupid questions or hassle involved, the tix even included taking pictures.

"What's up with this guy? Why is he so happy about taking pics and stuff?"- A valid question among the younger readers who grew up with a smartphone. See, we are talking about 1990 and at that time there was no standardized citizen with a smartphone. The small, cheap, sometimes hideable one way cameras, which fans tried to sneak in to the gig, were basically not allowed. Let's mention that it was hopeless for anybody with decent camera equipment to enter the show unless he had the allowance of the band or the tour-promoter.so this was a real privilege for me to make pics of the bands playing. Fortunately I was in the position to have a decent camera, still lacking any photographic skills though.at least I was ready to shoot for the first time ever.

The opening shot at that right was absolutely insane, a huge hammer that blew me away, DEMOLITION HAMMER. I had never heard anything about those guys but their song material made it somehow, I really liked the stuff these guys from New York were pouring out. These were my first ever legal shots which made it on film!

In addition to the allowance of doing this and that during a concert, one of the best things to happen was the fact that I could pass this dark and dreadful looking security wall into the backstage area. Those living towers at the entrance to this sacred area had to keep their sticky fingers in their pants. Our Promoter was a well-known personality and she was the one who made it possible for us to enter the magic realm of the rockstars. In our case it was a very small room, white walls, a table and a few chairs. On the way to it we found tons of empty beer cases and accessories belonging to the club. Actually not the kind of glamour we were thinking of-welcome to reality. Some really important dudes were crowding the few left, dried out sandwiches where the cheese was already bending towards the sky like a dying vulture in the desert, spreading out its wings for a final time. Among this desperate looking crowd I spotted a few faces which I only knew from record-covers. In those times it was something really special to be so close to guys you never had a chance to see in real, no YOUTUBE or anything else involved created this very special moment…it was like magic somehow.

The interview we had with James Murphy who was with OBITUARY? Was all in all a non-typical interview for a small, unexperienced fanzine? Embarrassing questions such as "when did you start the band" or" what's the meaning of your bands' name" were an absolute no go for Sascha. With my profound lack of English-knowledge at that time I was merely able to catch a bit here and there, speaking this language was beyond my reach at that time, don't forget how young and shy I was, hahahahaha. Sascha instead was the guy to just speak and understand, as if this was his native language. James, who was with DEATH as a guitarist a few months ago, chatted with Sascha about his ex-boss Chuck Schuldiner and all the arguments they had, his fast move to OBITUARY and the creative progress leading into their new release "Cause of Death".

When we finally said goodbye I had this crazy thought for a moment, right after the handshake:" omg maybe you will never wash your hand again?"

I took more pics that evening and was absolutely happy. OBITUARY! Wow, what an onslaught, amazing!!!!I was lucky enough to see the first drummer who performed those ultra-doublebass-attacks with bare feet, big cinema!!!!!!!!!!!!!!!

MORGOTH: The reigning band at the end of the day. They were know at that time as the most professional wrecking crew of the country, that was something nobody could take away from those guys, the ruled the place. Without a doubt: A more than deserving Headliner. Marc Grewe who did vocals and bass at that time, was screaming at the top of his lungs and the band surrounding laid out the perfect carpet for the ultimate mayhem. What an amazing evening with some really really good bands.

This was definitely an experience, my first time!!!!!

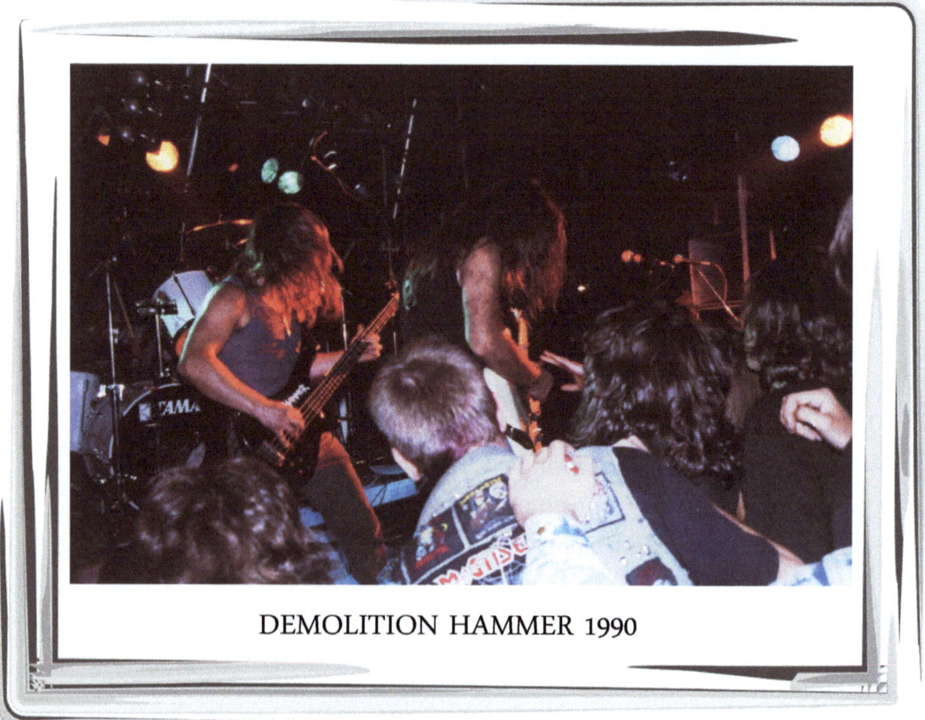

DEMOLITION HAMMER 1990

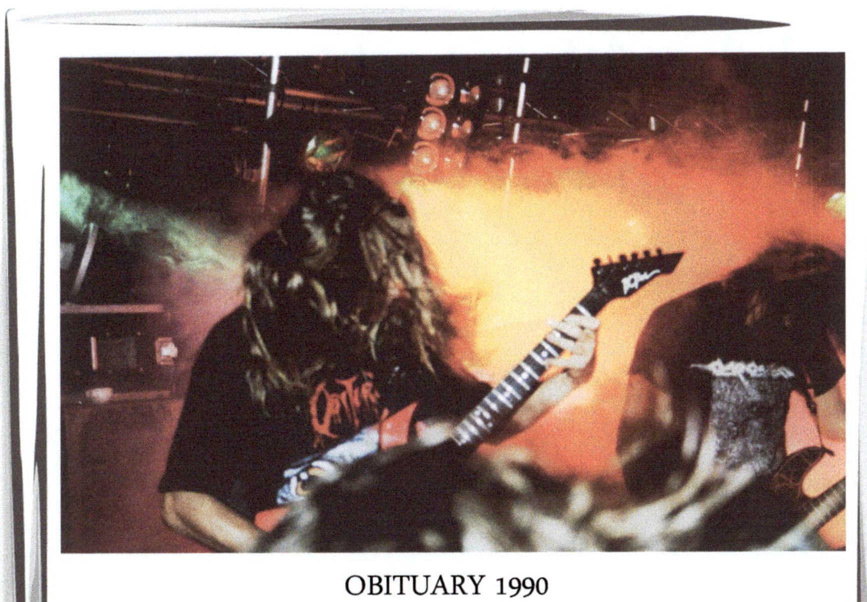

OBITUARY 1990

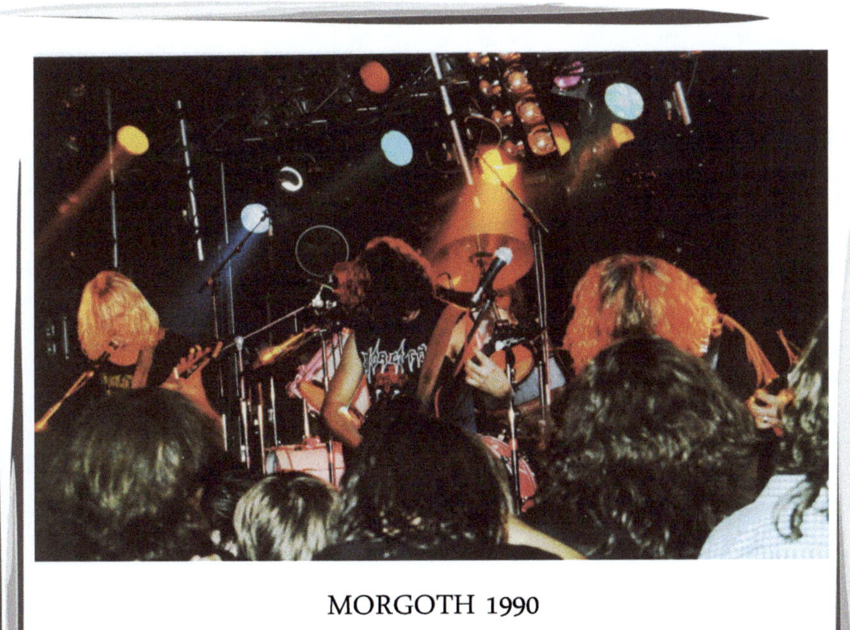

MORGOTH 1990

GAMMA RAY

and the rescue of the blood cans

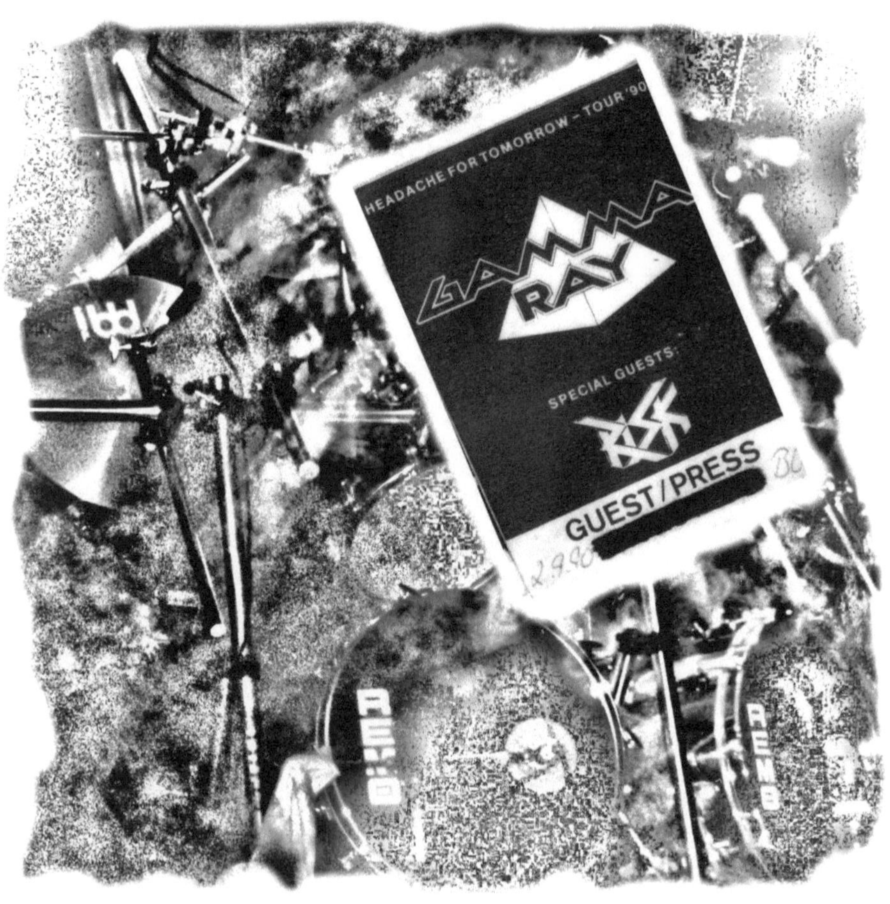

Sascha was very happy with the first pics we took, which meant for me that I was part of the crew now. Freelance photoguy for a mag dealing with my passion: heavy metal!

The next job came in pretty fast: GAMMA RAY were supposed to play a gig in Bochum, the tour was called "Headache for Tomorrow!" Since Sascha was unable to attend the show I got a new partner, her name was Martina and we both had the honorable task to take the interview with the headliners.

On the Autobahn A52, especially on the first part between Düsseldorf and the location of the gig in Bochum, there was always this looming danger of traffic jams. Right here, where three lanes connected into one, the first drama of the day was bound to unfold. Martina was always on fire, very exhausting to say so. She drove me nuts with her impatience and constant changing of cassettes, feeding the cassette player in the car.

Bang!!! A loud, irritating sound of grinding metal and the feeling you have when you stop your car from 15mph to zero in a split-second, we made it into the trunk of a car right in front of us. It was an new Opel. My car was a borrowed one from my friend Thomas. There you go...This was all not really cool. The guy from the other car was really friendly but seemed quite unrelaxed somehow. His rear door didn't look too good and he could not close it anymore, it was more of a dangling around piece of debris than what it was supposed to be before the impact happened. The reason for his discomfort was plain and simple: he was transporting blood cans!!!

So we got the VW Golf off the tracks to see it the valuable freight made it unfazed by the impact-and Strike!!! We were lucky! The cans looked ok and so we exchanged our insurance data. Right after this we tried for at least 15 minutes to somehow connect his deranged hatch to the rest of his car, since he had to continue his trip to the next hospital somehow. My friend's car looked not so bad, headlights and front grill were damaged but back in the day it was way easier to fix such things by yourself, which enabled me to repair the car myself and so, ultimately avoiding an expensive body shop, which also reduced the anger of my good buddy Thomas.

The rest of the trip was way calmer than before, guess why? Arriving at the Zeche Bochum we saw a lot of people running around from left to right and in return, things were busy already it seemed. Off to get the Press pass and the Photo pass. Unlike to my first gig in cologne with MORGOTH I found myself standing in a big pit, really professional looking stuff to say so. The Pit has its own rules to say so, which was something I had to learn in the concerts to follow, today there was none of these rules existent.

There were like ten other photographers in the pit, since this place was really not too crowded I found myself quite comfortable standing in the 1st row without being squeezed to death. The tour guests, which were a German band called RISK played a very solid set featuring their hit from the days "Ratman". All in all they were enjoyable and I wished for a longer set, which did not come true.

Kai Hansen and his crew had the audience completely under control during the whole set as the headliner for today "Helloween". Right at the end the played the fan-favorite song "Starlight" and the crowd exploded.

Oh man, when the gig was over I so wanted to go home, since I had to get up at 6 am and there was also the damaged car waiting for me. Instead I found myself waiting for the band and the interview, which was slated after the band had a shower and some food, this took some time...

Martina held the Interview and she was really excited when she asked the band all those questions which were a no-go actually and I thought to myself OMG!!!!!!!!!!!!!!!!!!

Returning home the repair of the car went really smooth and easy with some pieces from the junkyard for roughly 50 Deutschmarks. So I made sure that the grim look on my buddy's face vanished into thin air and he finally approved the whole repair. After that incident I avoided asking Thomas about giving me his car as the interview-cab to say.

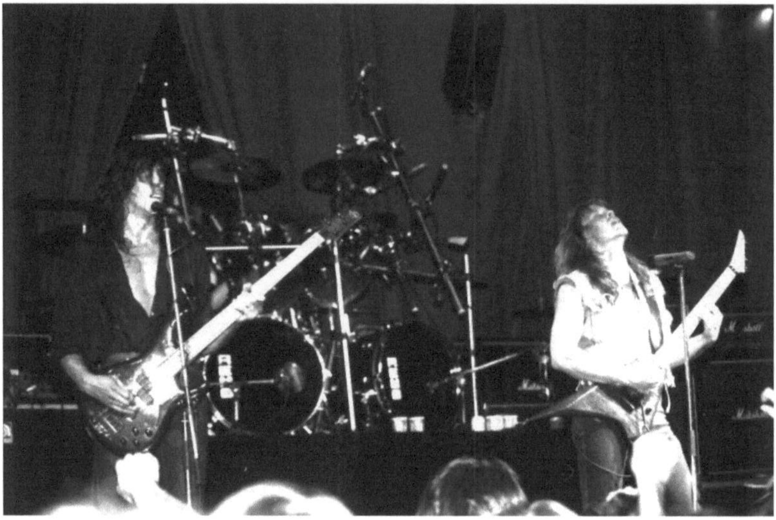

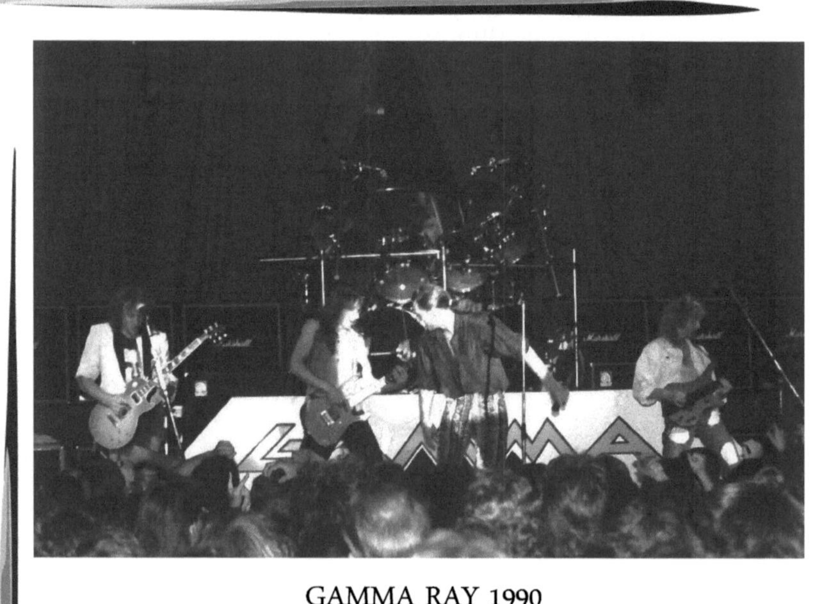

RISK 1990

GAMMA RAY 1990

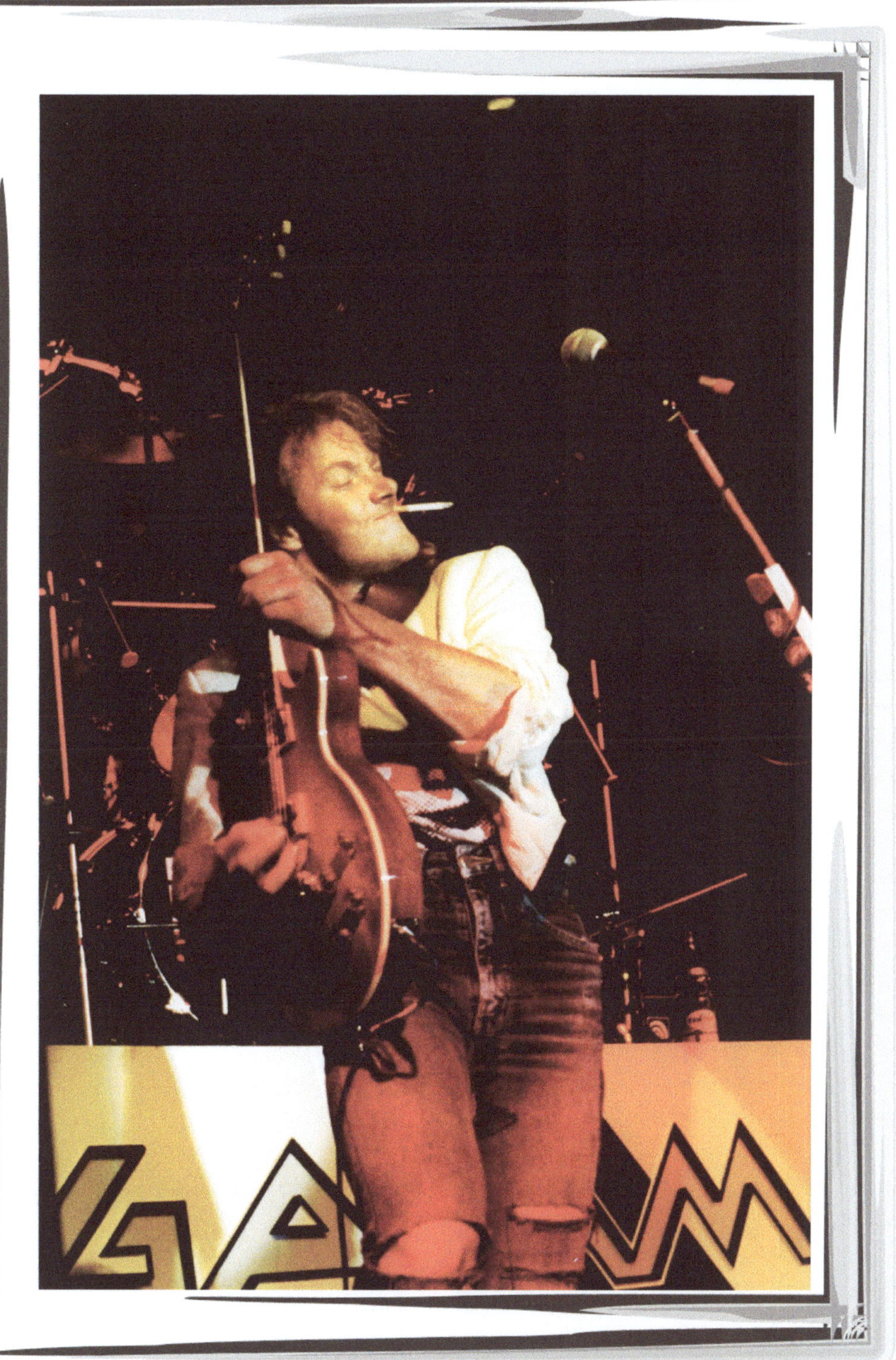

KAI HANSEN 1990

24-7 SPYZ

...spies everywhere

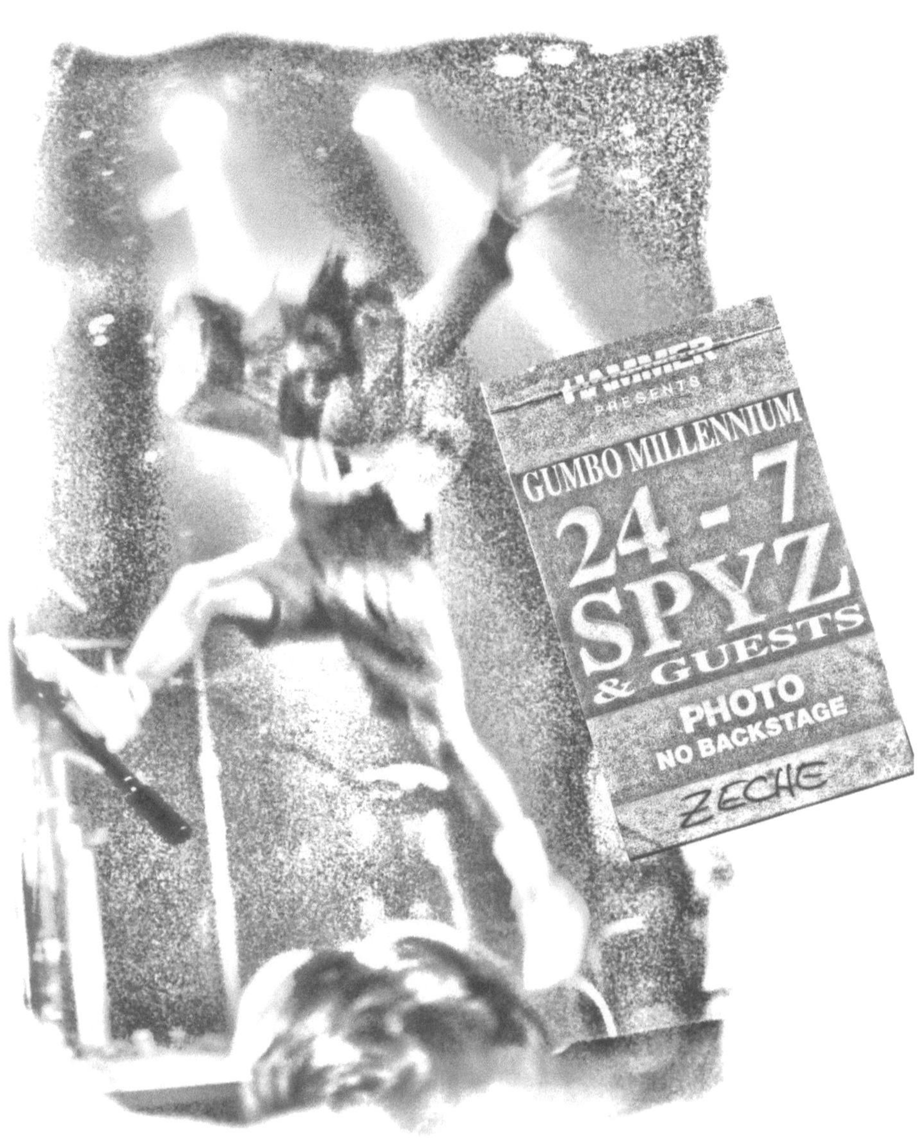

Sascha had new tasks on his agenda shortly after the gig and so it was again the Autobahn A52 and again the Zeche Bochum, this time with the bossman himself and no accidents. Some guys from the US were playing that night, they had a very unusual band name called "24-7 SPYZ". Never heard anything about these guys, so a surprise gig was bound to happen in a few. Sascha was the man with the ultimate knowledge, when we arrived he jumped the tour-bus immediately and I saw a few Bob Marley lookalikes leaving the bus at that moment. They had baseball shirts and jeans and looked so typically American. Approaching these guys I only understood nothing, since their slang-they came from the Bronx, sounded like a mixture of John Wayne and a mouthful of chewing gum. These black guys spoke the way they were used and I was completely out of the game for today. Sascha instead did a great interview with these folks since he was an exchange student a couple of years ago and for him it was an easy game talking with these guys.

Their funk-metal mix was well appreciated by the audience that evening, the place was crowded!! What I didn't know at that time, was the fact, that these dudes had already sold over 100,000 copies of their current album, well you are never too old to learn something...

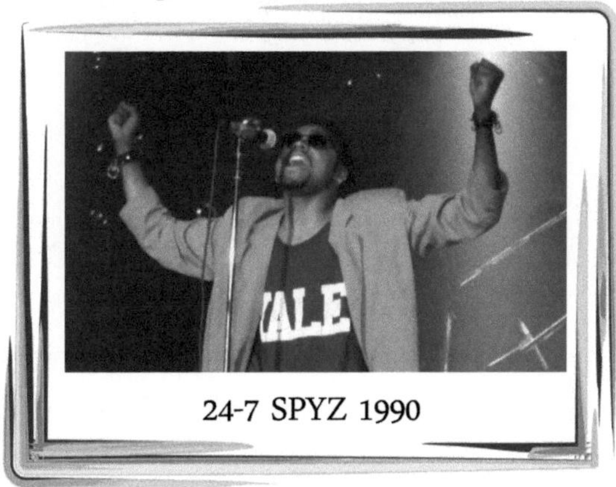

24-7 SPYZ 1990

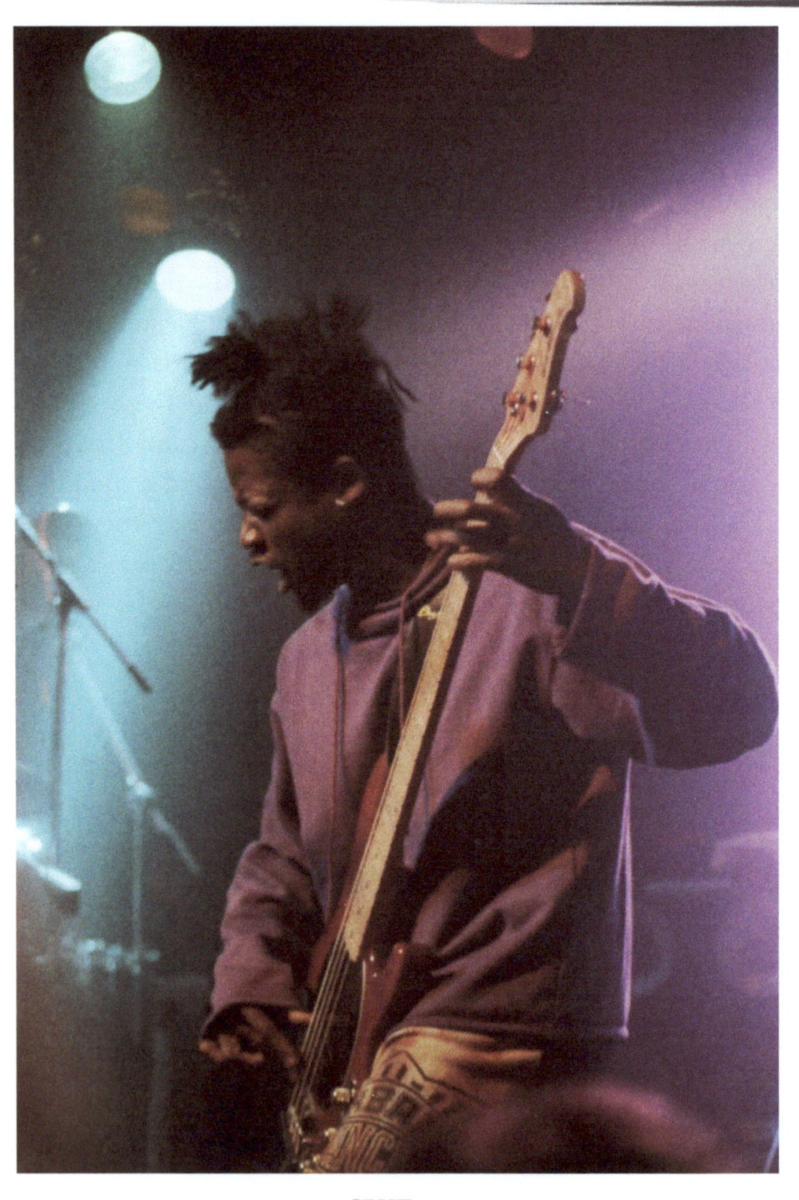

24-7 SPYZ 1990

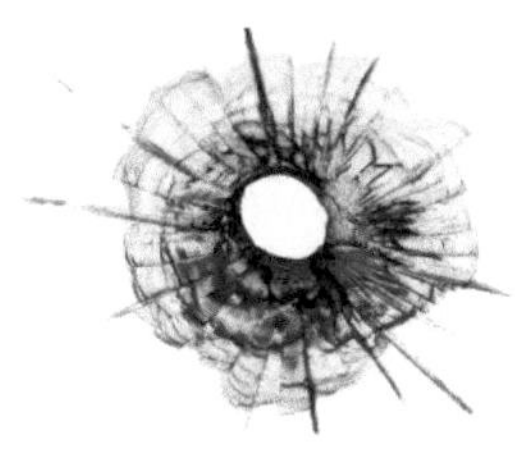

THIS ONE I WANT,
THIS ONE NO...

During those days of constant driving around from gig to, Sascha provided us with tons of of promo-tapes and cds, we were literally drowning in that stuff, when we had one of our rare editorial staff meetings. Since we were limited in the number of pages we could actually review and print, the "boss" decided what was to be reviewed and what not. That was the first step into dependency for us. Since we received all this stuff for free the labels or companies wanted to see feedback as a review, a positive review is the best thing for future samples to come. This comes close to the fact that this is the first step to kill the initial thought of criticizing what you like and what not.

So one thing lead to another...When you defend your ideals and ignore stuff the companies want to be pushed you are bound to loose the support of the companies. This also means less support with advertisements, which ultimately leads into the bowels of nirvana. Since the job started to make fun the decision of morals aspects had been shed aside in the beginning. Sascha was a supercool guy anyway and he seemed unfazed form any grief or existential thoughts coming from the fact that publishing a mag also means great responsibility. "No, no, I didn't sell out"

Now, in the aftermath I have these thoughts haunting me from time to time. Back in the day I really didn't give a shit about that kind of thoughts. We were all happy with our job and nothing else mattered. We promoted the one and only music style and were fortunate enough to have a way deeper experience, than a lot of others, that's legit, ain't it?

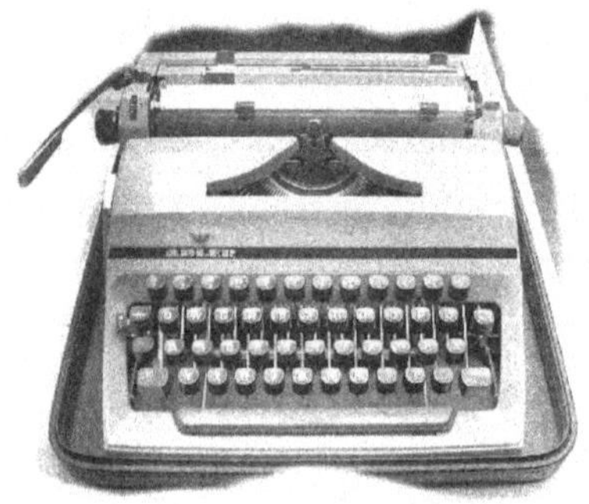

The office of the chief-editor 1990

WHITESNAKE

Poison and other Giants

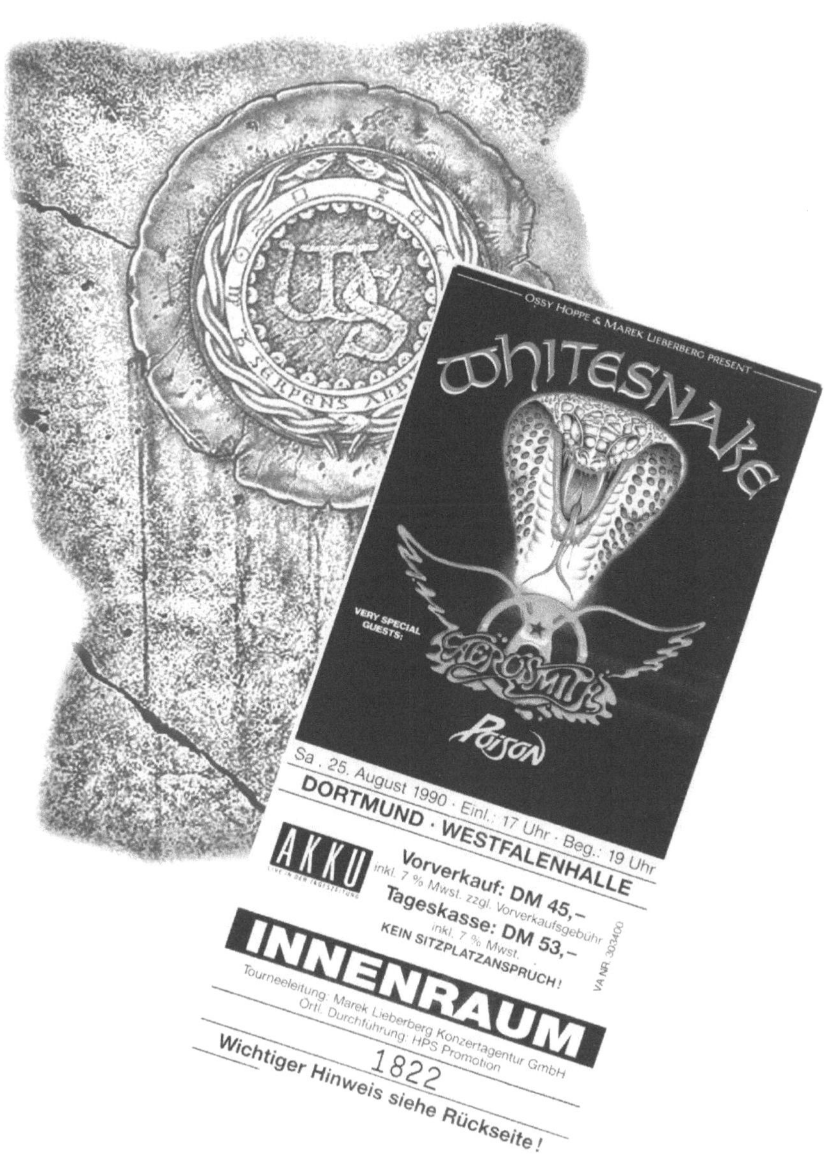

Without a doubt our schedule filled up with more and more work and fun. So my duties as a photographer shifted more and more to things which had nothing to do with my main profession. The Westfalenhalle 1 Dortmund was the place to go for another epic gig, which we were supposed to feature in our next mag. No pictures allowed, well, that was a clear message!

"Holli...we need a live-review, and now get going!"

Mhhhhh, very unpleasant.

POISON, AEROSMITH, and WHITESNAKE playing at august, 25th, 1990, all in one gig and in our region, yippieehhhh!!!! 14,000 fans made it there and that was a huge crowd at that time. POISON were a band I absolutely did not prefer on my playlist. Glam-metal or posers never made the cut for me. The only tolerable song in their set was "every rose has its thorn". However, those wig-wearing guys were running up and down the huge stage and the audience really liked their show.

AEROSMITH was next as support for David Coverdale. A few years later this would not have happened, the other way around yes! Steven Tyler and his band lived up for the immaculate professionalism and showed everyone how 20 years rock 'n' roll business work.

WHITESNAKE, which were a top act at that time with their epic hits such as "Here I go again" or "Is this love?" delivered an unforgettable show. Not really astounding as the band consisted of extremely skilled musicians from that time surrounding David Coverdale: Steve Vai, Adrian Vandenberg, Rudy Sarzo, and Tommy Aldridge.

This all-star band was above any kind of doubt. Each of the musicians had the freedom to perform his solo skills during the set, which was an amazing combination with the complete show.

VENOM

and the wrath of the cult

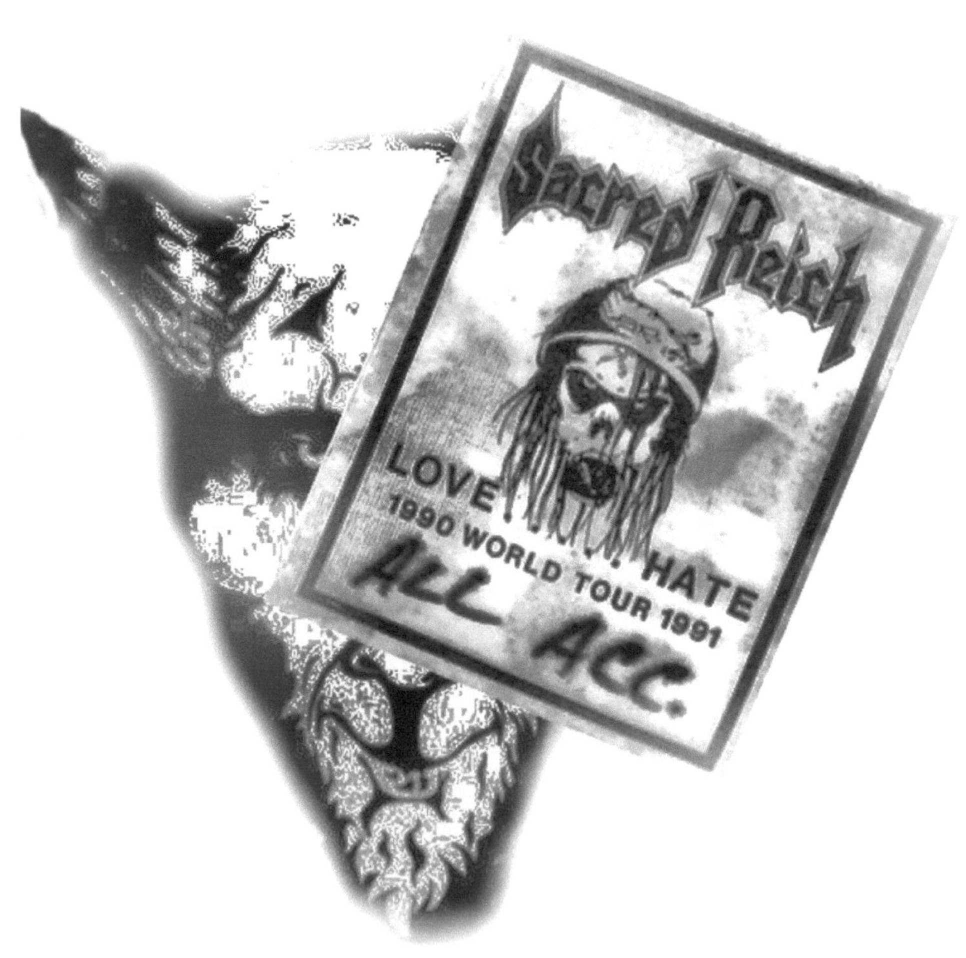

How fast times change.... My last VENOM, where I attended as a fan, was quite some time ago, but I was still under the impression from that night. Back then, in the year 1985 VENOM rivaled METALLICA as the headliner for the Metal Hammer Festival at the Loreley and the swung their dark hammer with an enormous thunder for the 15.000 fans attending. A bombastic show par excellence, which helped me forget the pain I felt in my feet after having stood for more than 14 hours during the concerts. Today it was a different game with TOR3 housing max 1000 fans and it wasn't a sold out show. Those five spots in the first three rows were no comparison to the light-avalanches the band used in the past. Everything came across really strange that day.

With their music and their way of presenting it to the audience during that time they surely had paved new ways for the bands to follow. Cronos, the front man, wasn't with the band during that time, since they ran into too many arguments. Instead of burying the myth a new shouter and a second guitarist joined the band. No ill will against the new blood, but it didn't bring anything. Certain special bands such as VENOM, who could have moved mountains with their extreme presence, should know when their time has come and call it quits. They should avoid to continue, just for the sake of it. But that's just how I feel about things.

It wasn't the fault of the new guys, that's for sure. The interview we had in their tour bus revealed all the necessary background info, brought a lot of fun, and the insight into plastic bathtubs filled with hard alcohol. Mantas, Abbadon,

Demolition Man and Co. never lacked the groupies either: Nevertheless we really had a good time with our heroes from the early days.

How fast paced the times were came to my attention a few years later, when the original line up presented a gigantic show in Eindhoven at the Dynamo-Festival. The guys had been quite busy in between. The cult surrounding the band ebbed a bit off during the time when Cronos was not with them, but it wasn't completely gone by far.

Oh yes, forgive me, also on tour were ATROPHY and SACRED REICH, with the first band Sascha had a small interview. At the same time I caught Phil Rind of SACRED REICH with my camera on stage where he got bombed by the fog-canon. Pretty sad that especially this band never really made it despite their cult hits "Surfing Nicaragua" or "The American Way", but well, that's life!

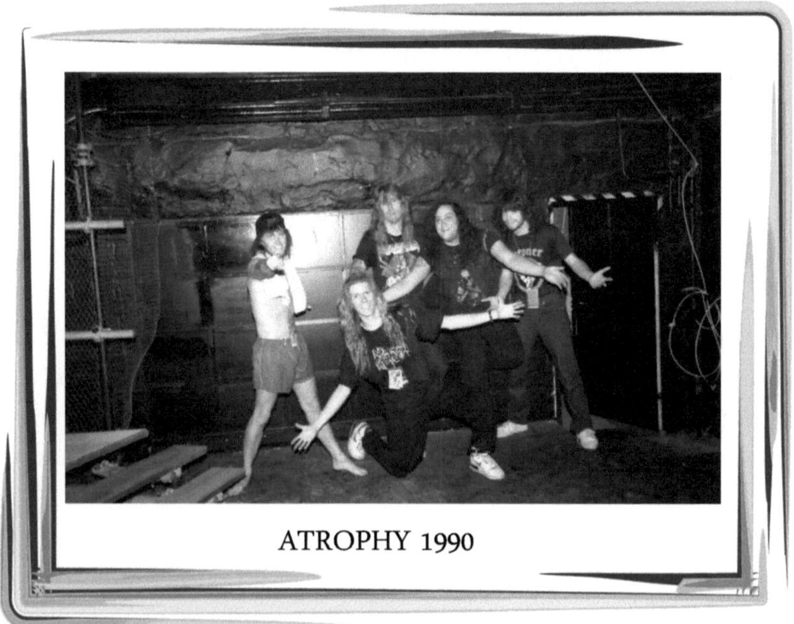

ATROPHY 1990

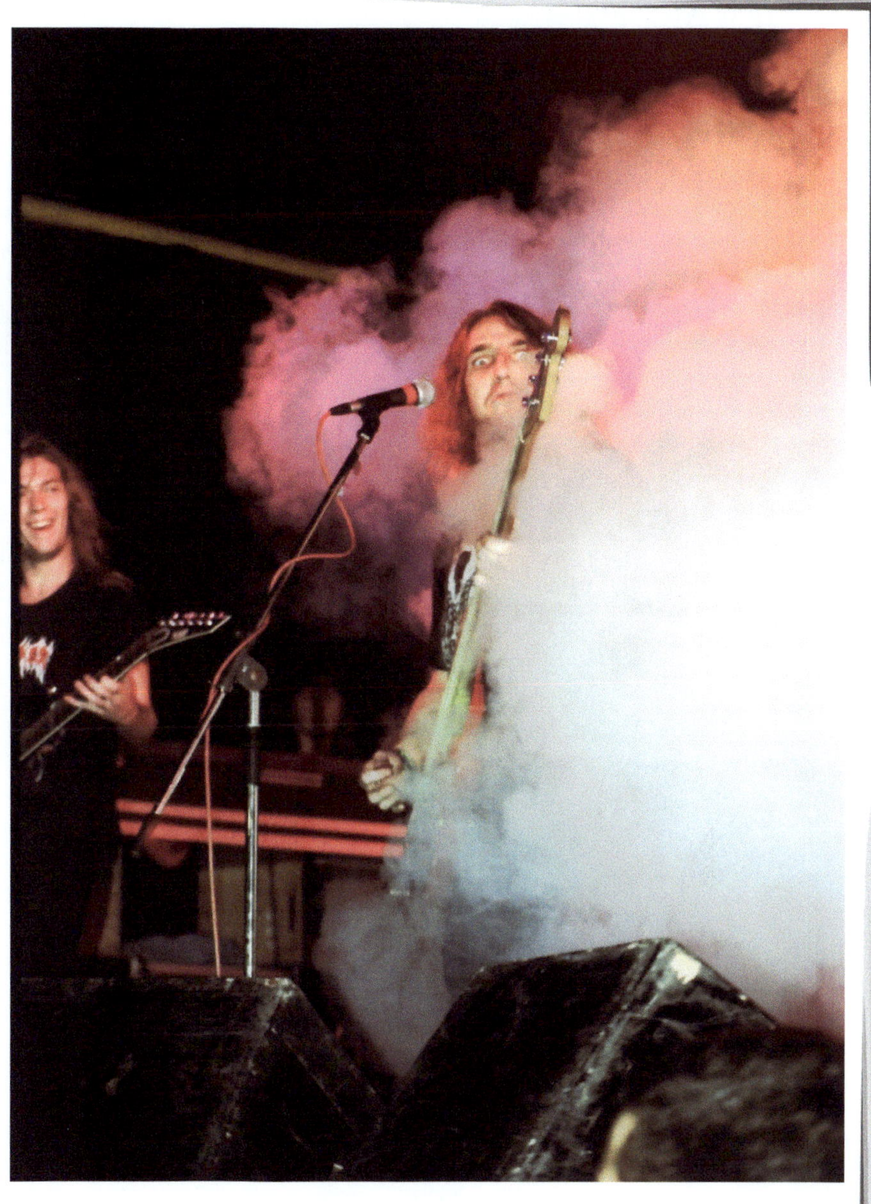

SACRED REICH 1990

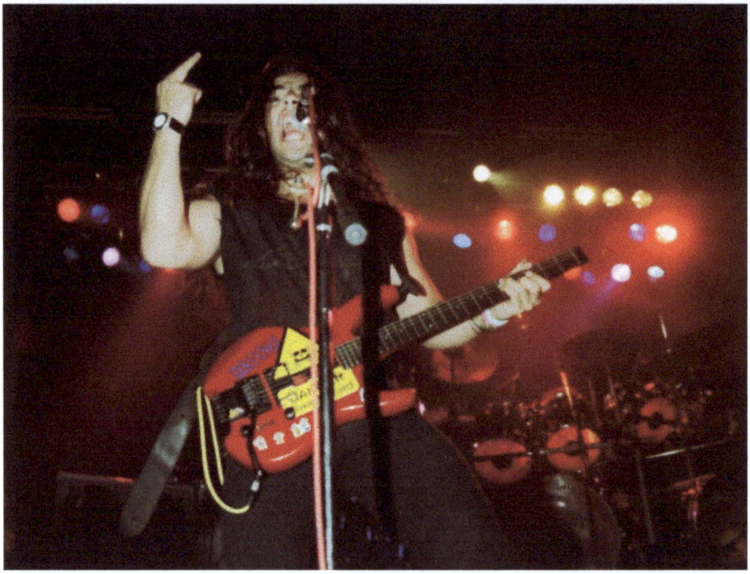

VENOM 1990

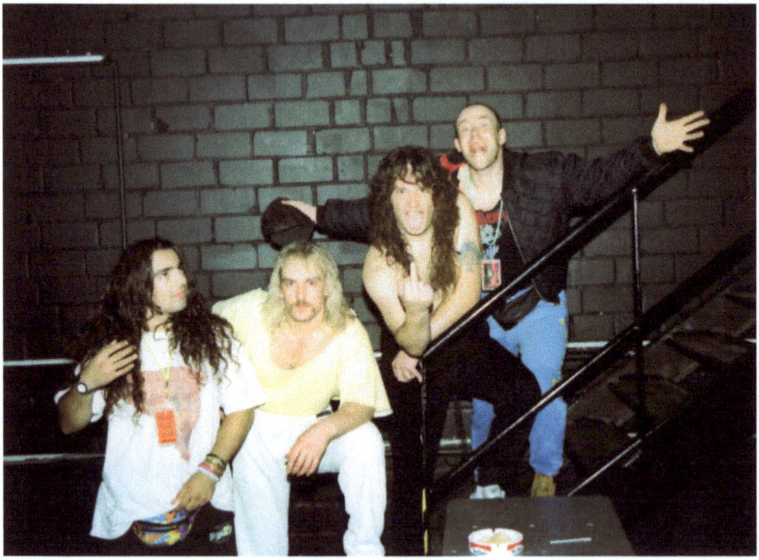

VENOM 1990

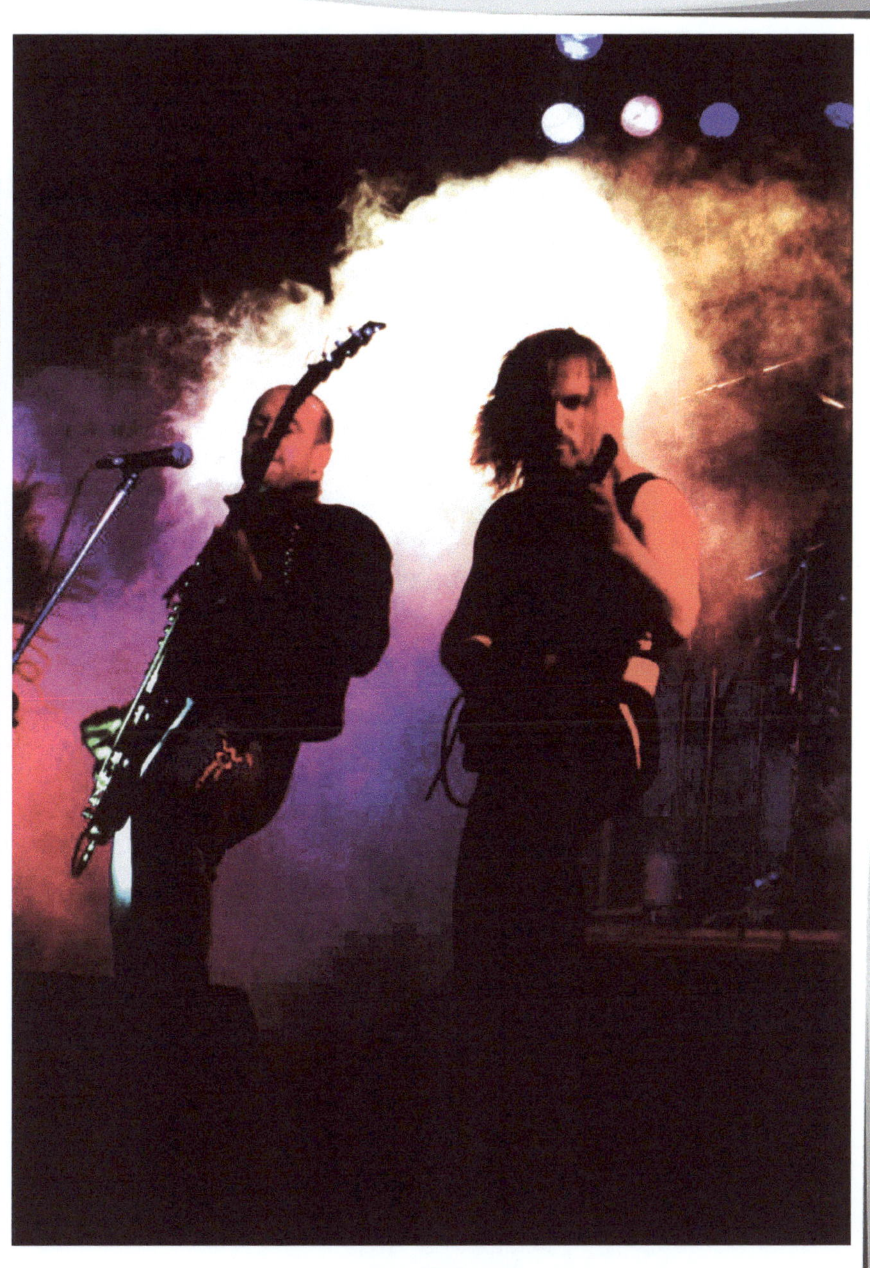

VENOM 1990

ANNIHILATOR

and the ghostbusters

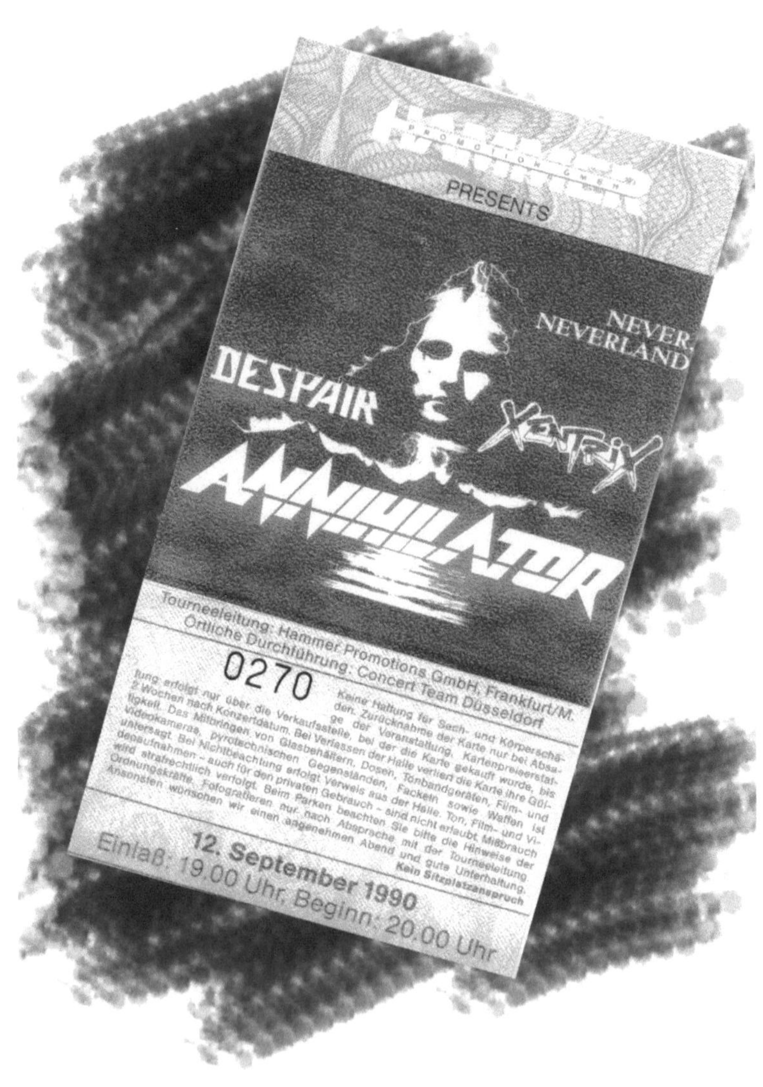

The bouncers at the TOR3 almost forgot to as us for our press passes during that time, since we seemed to be inventory already. Since my buddy Thomas was the photographer for the day, I enjoyed myself with a couple beers and enjoyed the view. Jeff Waters and his crew were on tour to promote their album "Never Neverland". Their guests were XENTRIX and DESPAIR. XENTRIX had that ghostbusters song at that time and that was all I knew about those guys. DESPAIR were at advantage since they played a hometown gig that night with their singer Thomas Henschel. He was with a local band called APOSTASY which was into bay area thrash metal. So that was something we had to see, since we want were eager to find out why he had left this really cool band. The guys from Dortmund called DESPAIR, with Waldemar Sorychta who later formed the project GRIP INC. with Dave Lombardo of SLAYER, didn't really make the cut that evening.

XENTRIX didn't have an easy spot either. At least their previously mentioned cover song convinced the audience for a short period.

ANNIHILATOR was the magic word of the evening. They turned the place upside down with their musical skills and ultimate precision including their joy of performing live. At that time "Never Neverland" was regarded as a very sterile production. In the here and now such productions happen on a daily base. Back then it took some time to get used to get acquainted to that kind of sound, nevertheless these guys killed it live.

CLASH OF THE TITANS

- Not for me!!!!!!!!!!!!!!!

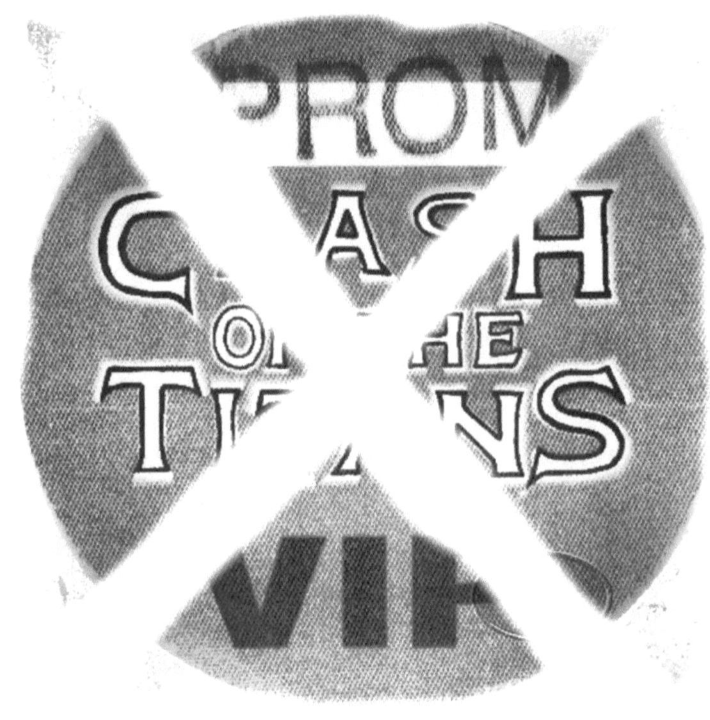

During one of our staff meetings Sascha's euphoria seemed to peak to the max when he got word that day, that his interview request for MEGADETH at today's legendary CLASH OF THE TITANS got ok'ed. This was not very common indeed. Such a small fanzine meeting such a big band was not a daily ritual. I, for myself, stayed rather skeptical when it came to that type of thing, but really didn't want to spoil his joy.

On Oct 6th 1990 Sascha called me: "Come on, pack your things, we really have the interview. It's going down at the Intercontinental Hotel at 2pm sharp."

Ok, let's do it then...

The lobby of the hotel was like a place from another world. That luxurious place presented itself in all its glamour. The best of furniture in the reception area combined with extremely expensive clad guests who strolled around at the entrance. What a sight. But wait, something was wrong with the picture, maybe their look at us longhaired no-goods when they saw us entering the place in our leather-jackets? NO! Wrong, absolutely wrong, we didn't make any effect, since the place was crowded with lookalikes.

This bunch of black leather-wearing metalheads paired against the expensive and bright ambience was somehow really strange to view. Sascha headed directly towards the promoter in charge. He got told that he was due for an interview with Marty Friedman in a few, where Sascha started to discuss silently, but determined with that guy. When he left, Sascha started to complain about God and the world. They had promised him an interview with Dave Mustaine, but well, I didn't really care at all. Come on, a talk with my guitar hero Marty Friedmann is at least as good as anything else. So I stayed shut and enjoyed the interview and seeing one of my heroes. Let's not forget to mention that I also played guitar at that time, but my skills were not worth mentioning.

Marty Friedmann was a newbie to the band and so the questions asked tended more and more towards playing guitar. Nick Menza, the MEGA-drummer, joined our illustrious round at the table and brought fresh air in the questioning round. We were out of time after twenty minutes, but Marty, Nick, and Sascha continued babbling about this and that, they had a good time for sure.

Then we saw the extremely noble looking couple in the lobby. The guests of that house behaved the way they looked. Way over the top, as written in the book. It wasn't only us who were fascinated by the sight. Well, the old couple marched towards the elevators waiting for the next one to arrive. We heard a "BINGGGG" and the next elevator opened its doors when the couple shrieked back as if they both had seen something awkward. Well, it was only: Dave Mustaine.

Quite in a hurry they jumped the next elevator which had just opened its gates to save them from doom. Everybody was laughing his ass off, either above or beyond the tables in the lobby and Dave's grin spelled it out loud.

The excellent cuisine from that hotel was actually too much for the "rockstars" and Marty asked us for a fast-food place. Since we came from that area, we knew exactly where the good places were and we kindly offered our company. Nick Menza joined our march and so I ended up walking among such greats through my hometown. Yesterday I was simply a fan and weekend-guitarist and now this. Crazy shit for sure!!!

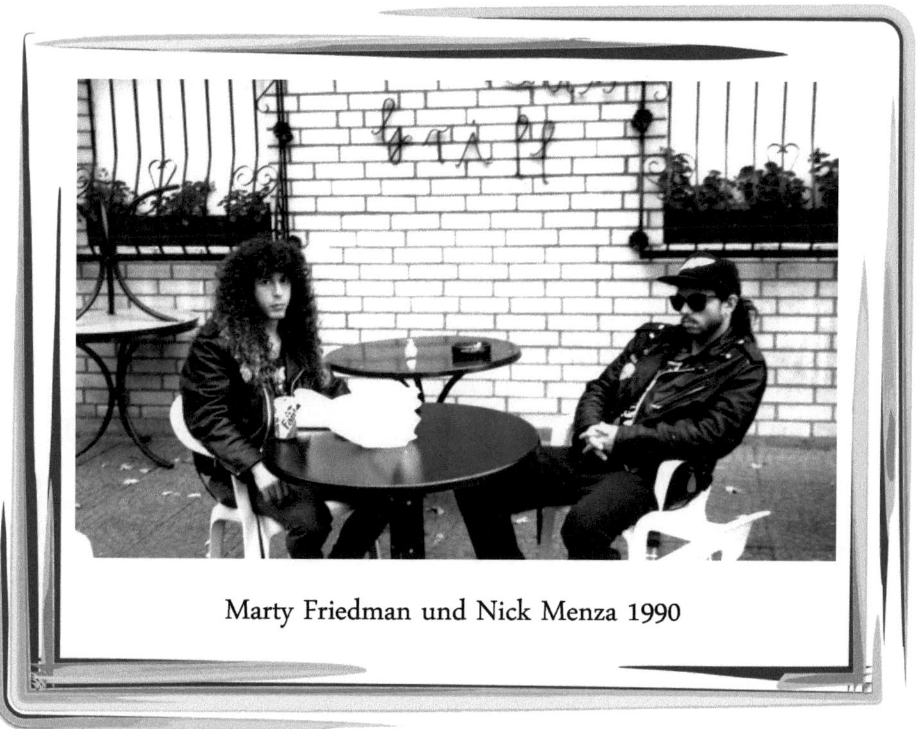

Marty Friedman und Nick Menza 1990

During our chitchat at the Nikolaus Grill a mom and her little daughter made it across the street, when a gigantic Rottweiler dog showed up and caught the pants of the little girl. The mother tried lifting the kid away from the dog, but to no avail. At the very same moment a young guy ran across the street towards the dog kicking into the animals sides, which led the dog to release his grip on the pants and then it just ran away, completely irritated. The actual owner of the dog was still out of sight and we just sat there, jaws dropped and being completely amazed by what we just witnessed.

The dog only wanted to play with someone!

The excitement didn't stop that day, more things yet to come for me.

The strong hand of reality struck at the very same night, when I was waiting for my photo pass and guess what, no photo pass for me. Sascha did his fire-dance, showing me that you have to fight for your right, which brought the promoter on the scene. He told us that we could gladly watch the show, but no pics tonight, which threw me, your loyal photoguy, into some problems. My valuable bag with all the camera stuff was not allowed to be taken inside.

Well, we had no car, no safe place to stash the stuff-the guy pointing towards his wristwatch, putting pressure on us, which meant that Sascha went inside and me...I went home!

Being out of cash at that time, I relied on the free entry, which was a grave mistake. I missed the legendary CLASH OF TITANS, this happened to me, the guy who was always there, well, this would never ever happen again.

MEKONG DELTA

The scare of your relatives

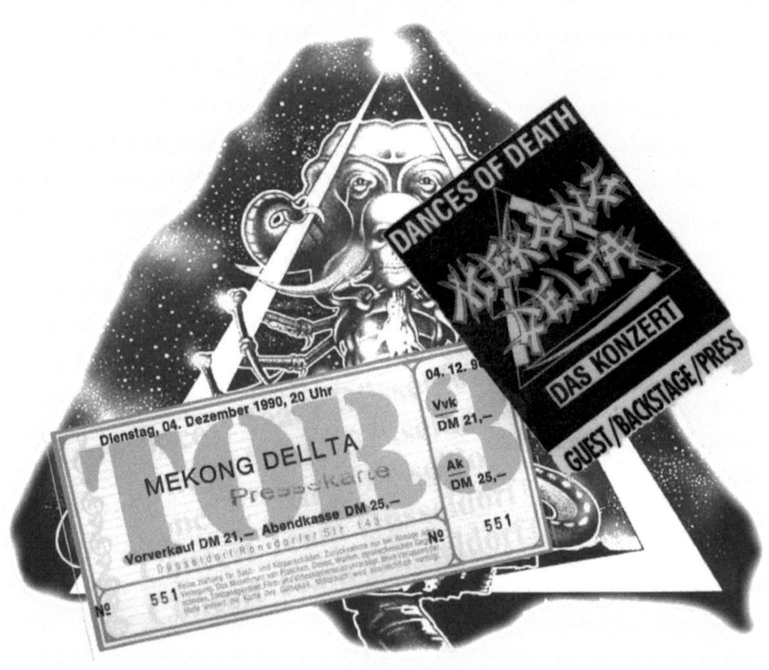

How times change.1990 the longplayer from MEKONG DELTA was an efficient thing to drive relatives out of your parents home, which is in 2014 unthinkable, since the relatives are listening to AC/DC or NIGHTWISH for example. Back then, this was a reason to be put into a children's ward when you listened to such devilish music at your home.

MEKONG DELTA had a special way to combine classic and thrash and they were quite unique at that time. The members of the band were something like a mystery due to contracts involved or due to the promotional effect. Today was the day for one of their rare appearances. Singer Doug Lee made it a very special evening with his way of playing with that mystery, too bad I couldn't take pics that evening. The following interview, the guitarist Uwe Baltrusch told me about their classical influences by Russian composers, such as Modest Mugorsky and Co.

Meanwhile it is a well-known fact who played alongside with the band boss Ralf Hubert aka Björn Eklund. Drums was Uli Kusch (GAMMA RAY, HOLY MOSES) aka Patrick Duval flowing the footsteps of Jörg Miachael (RUNNING WILD) aka Gordon Perkins.

For sure one of the most extraordinary and most underrated bands coming from Germany.

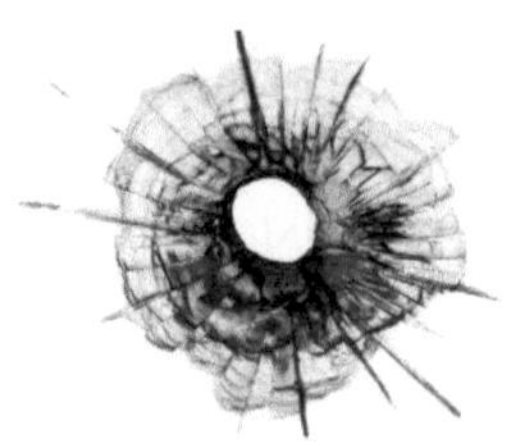# The Future is now, or:

The rush of science

Slowly but steady we had a certain routine creeping into our spare time project. When you had no gigs to attend you ended up doing reviews of the Prome MC's —or CD's.

I, for myself, was so sick and tired of the old-age gluing and copy and paste stuff, which always led to a bad print result. You work your ass off with the content and in the end nobody can decipher what you wrote. So I obtained a program for my Amiga 500, which helped me to do page layouts and all of a sudden the modern world swung its doors wide open, at least partially. Still scary compared to todays' possibilities. After a short time I was looking at my very first page created with the system and I thought this was the shit. It looked quite decent. But how do I check the result? Or how do I get this on paper? I ended up buying tons of mags, went to a couple of stores and gathered information which finally led to the purchase of a 24 needle printer with a resolution of 300 dpi. This was a dream come true for only 500 deutschmarks. OUCH!!!!!!!!!!!!!!!!

Printing on a black and white laser printer was out of reach, since the price was tripled then.

As a trainee in 1991 this was steep. Whatever, I enjoyed my hobby and bought that thing. We often freak out when the internet sucks and the speed is too low, back then, during the times of the Commodore Amiga 500,with 2m work space, this was quite a different game. If you wanted to print a single page with a few graphics but no pics you had suffer from tremendous noise, created by the printer, for at least 20 minutes per page. In the beginning you sat next to the printer, eagerly waiting for the result, but after some time the pain in your ears convinced you to leave and take a snack at the next junk food parlor.

This worked in most cases, unless that piece of shit printer decided to swallow a sheet. But...if you want want it nice and clean you have to suffer a bit, isn't that the saying?

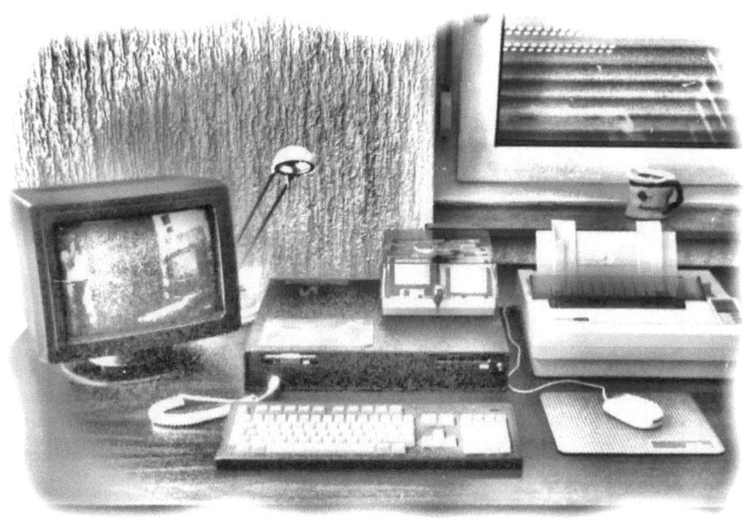

Hollis Amiga hightech Office 1991

DEICIDE

and the forces of justice

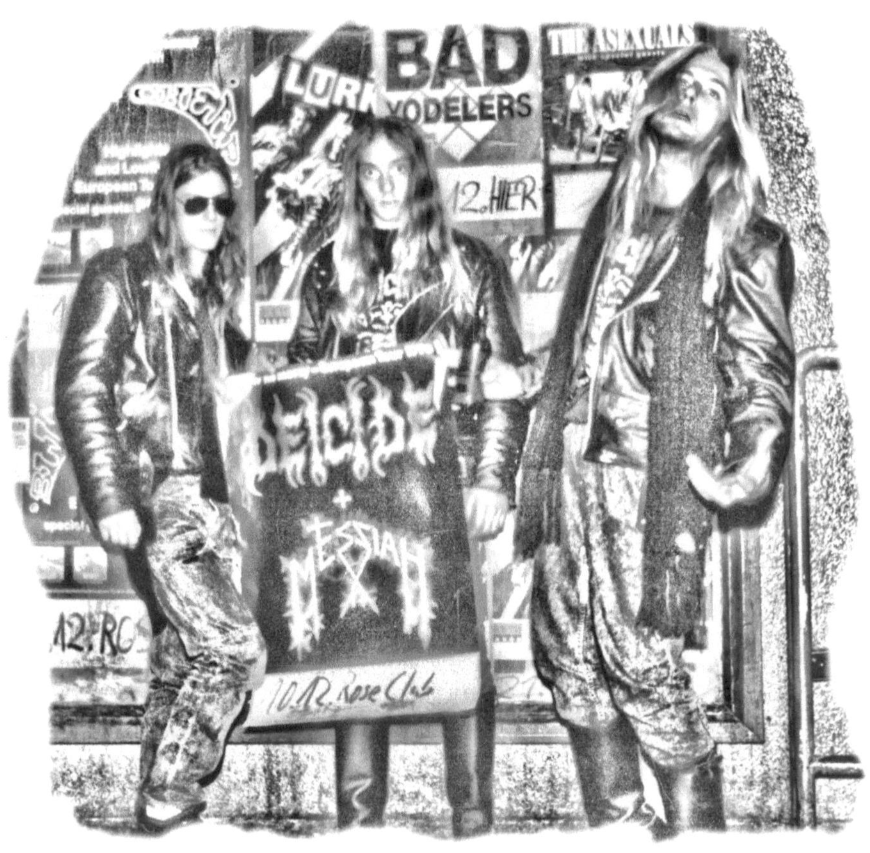

"Let's go to the enemy's city", Sascha joked on the phone one night.

"We go to Cologne, DEICIDE and MESSIAH play tonight. "Such a great band playing in a small club called the Rose Club, that's what I thought and I was sure the place would be packed. But when we arrived, the doors were wide open and nobody was there. We saw the girl which already had promoted MORGOTH, coming towards us along with Glen Benton. He was pissed for sure, you could tell by the looks on his face and he was barking with his loud voice in the room, which sent a tingle down your spine. The promoter barely held against the strong wind coming out of his mouth and the frontman just left the room with his waving black hair and the upside down tattooed cross on his forehead. The guitarists were standing in the background looking really grim following their master with their eyes, when he left. So Sascha asked the two guys where Glen was going. They said: "He's going to kill somebody."

With a grin on their faces they told us the story and why everything was not as it was supposed to be. The tour-bus got raided by the customs when they tried to enter Germany. Since it was already 7 pm everybody was afraid to call the show off for tonight, but after a short phone conversation with the agent, this got confirmed. The bus was held in custody at the border, since they were under suspicion to carry drugs, so "No show tonight"

F....this, let's head home.

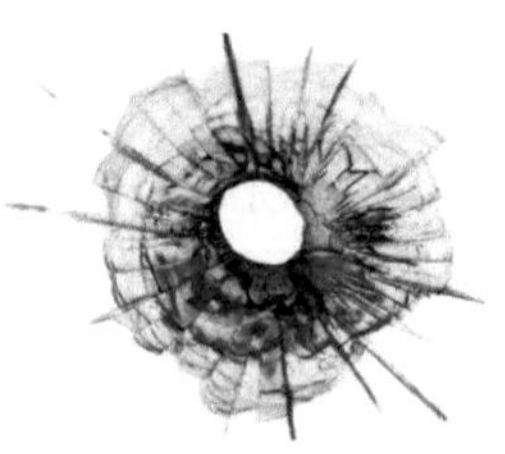

The Messiah just hung up

The crazy weeks continued on and on. You couldn't skype back then, which meant, if you wanted to do an interview with the rockstar of your likings and he was not within reach, to say so, you had to do the interview with a phone. This gave the record companies some work, since everything needed to be coordinated. It was a logistic masterpiece to get both parties together for an interview, completely different from the here and now. The interview was supposed to be cheap, no big expenses! Talking 20 minutes with somebody from the USA meant an invoice of 60 deutschmarks, there you go!!!!

Sascha had the pleasure to interview the, hmmm, let's say-completely crazy-THE GREAT KAT per phone. She played violin and brought her skills to a guitar. She had a freaky video clip called METAL MESSIAH, which brought a lot of attention. During her weird press-conferences she spilled out quite some crazy stuff, which led to the conclusion that she actually was a weirdo.

So, during their first phone interview, where Sascha, after having greeted her professionally, asked a critical question, things just happened. Beep. That was a cheap call for sure, the crazy guitar chick just hung up after a hearty "Fuck You".

These days, she wouldn't shock anybody anymore with her crazy way of representing herself, back then she was quite an appearance and stamped as crazy. Looking at it now, she just had a very extroverted way and a strong ego.

Bammmmm!

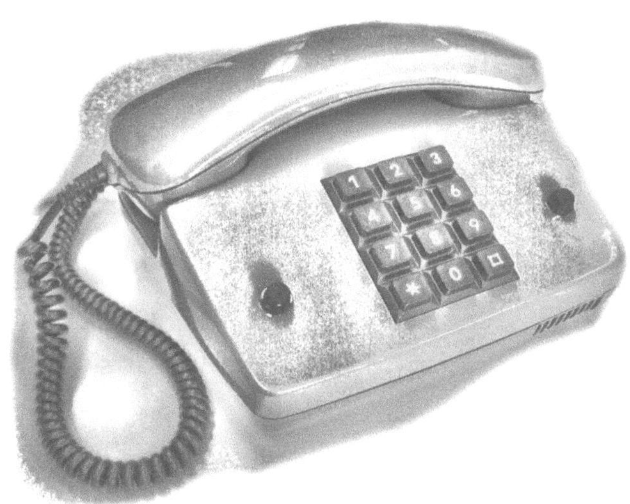

the telephone of my boss

KREATOR

and the very evil Chuck

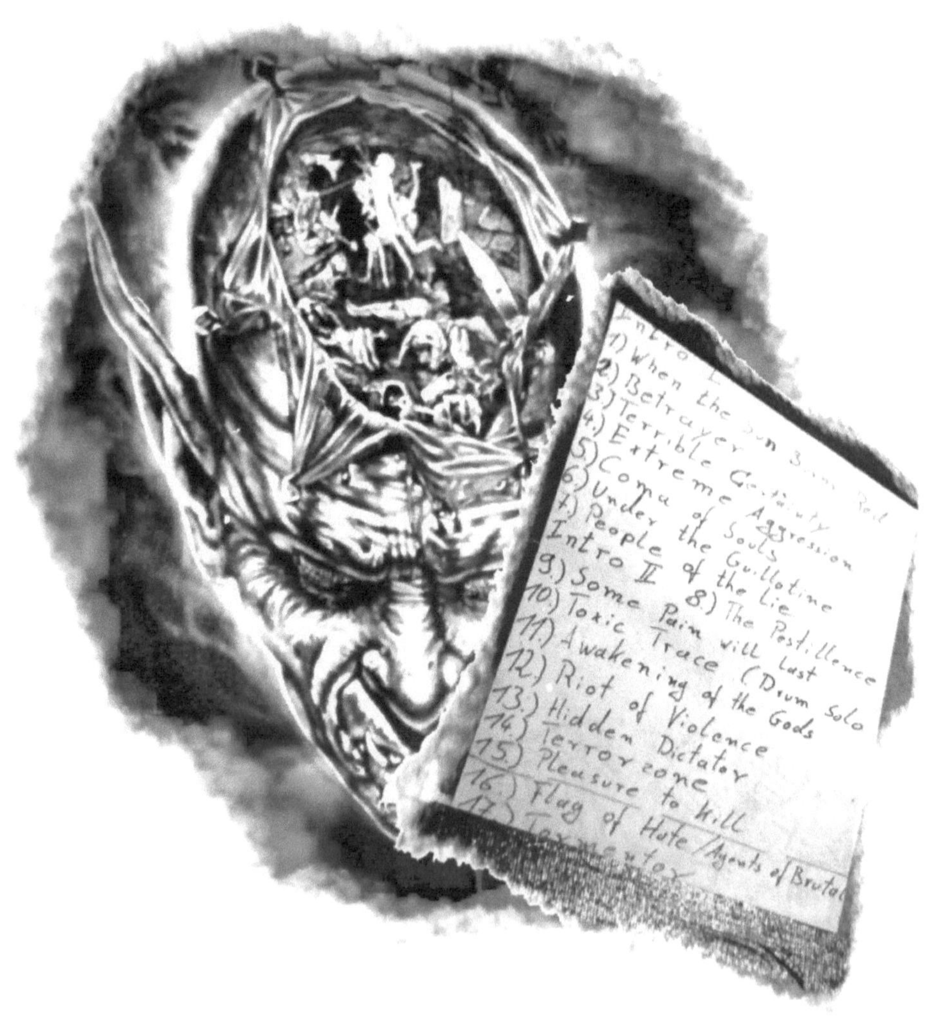

When there is need, us Fanziners and Fanzinerettes, long journey are done to provide the reader with interesting content. So this journey led us to Osnabrück to a place called Halle Gartlage. KREATOR, DEATH, and PROTECTOR were nesting there today, during their tour in order to shake some heads up at the show. Sascha somehow made it via some strange ways, to get in touch with the set-designer. He was interested in getting his stage shot prior to the show, for his references, and so they struck a deal, giving us the chance to satisfy his needs.

When our new team-member Diana approached Mille from KREATOR, to squeeze some info out of him, I did my job and took pics of the setting and the stage, which meant the world today.

Just one hour later the place was getting crowded and PROTECTOR were opening under the sign of 80's metal-bashing. Fitting for the first band of the show, their appearance was short-lived. Half an hour is a short time, even when fans liked what they saw.

Prior to the tour there was a lot of ruckus surrounding Chuck Schuldiner (R.I.P.) who was the DEATH-boss and who did not want to go on tour. After long struggles the band decided to tour without him, completely whack!!!

So the lights went out and DEATH were there with their placebo singer Rodney Dunsmore of DEVASTATION. They started to complain about their missing boss on stage and chanted "FUCK CHUCK"-choirs, which made the masses follow, but in the end it was a gig without any soul.

KREATOR showed the audience that night how the hammer in Essen swings and added a healthy portion out of their new album called "Coma of Souls".

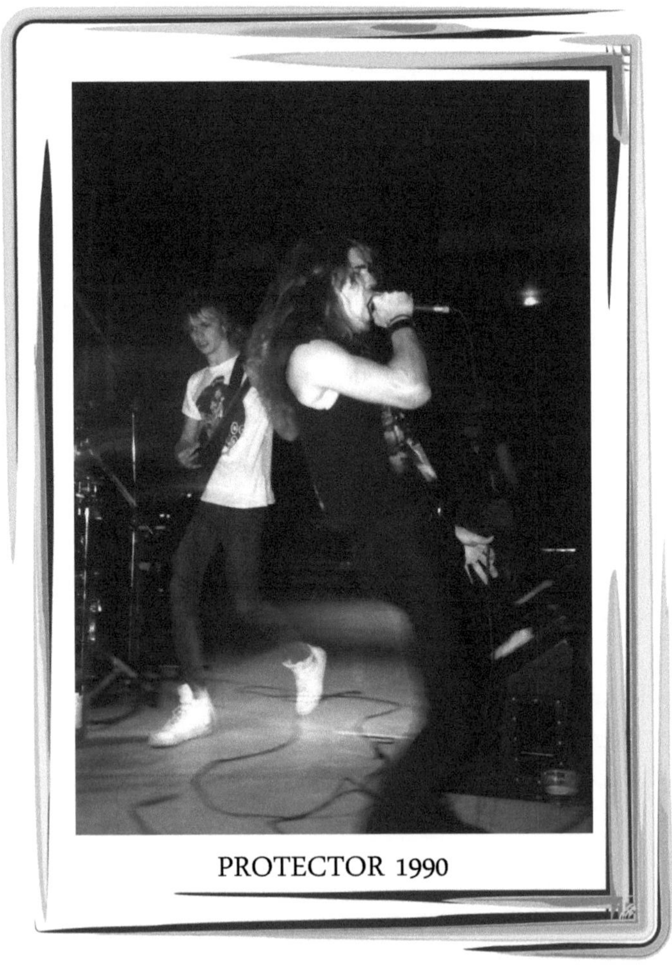

PROTECTOR 1990

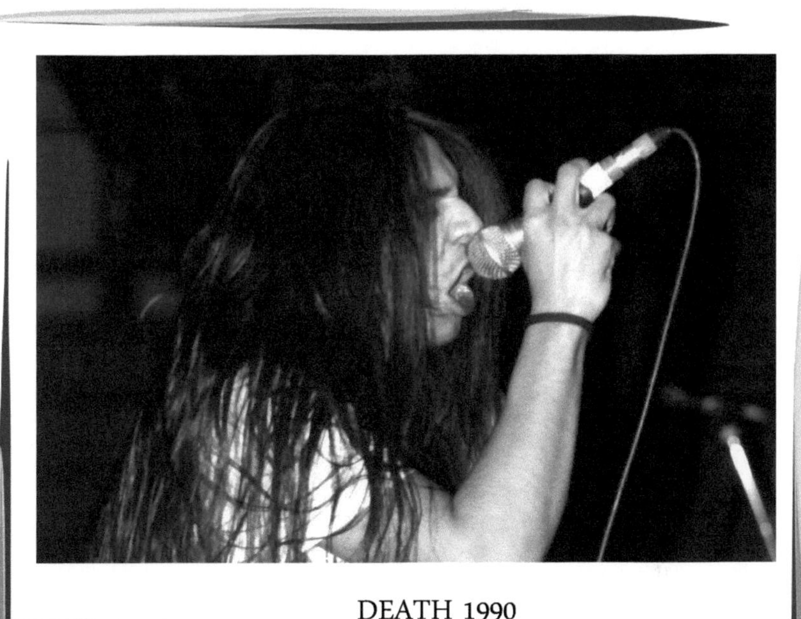

DEATH 1990

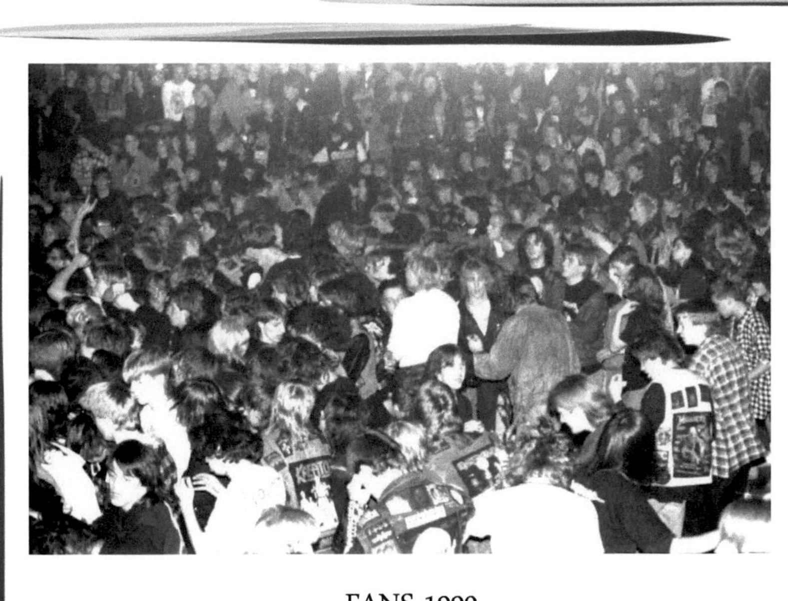

FANS 1990

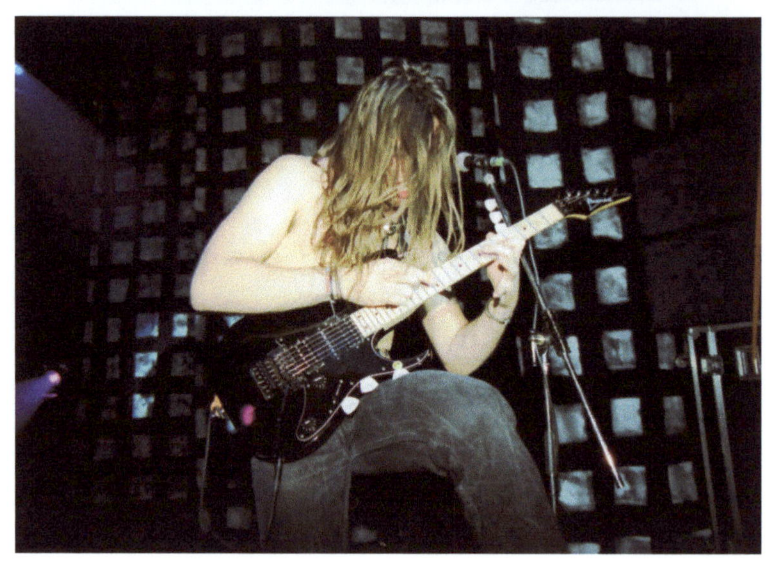

FRANK BLACKFIRE 1990

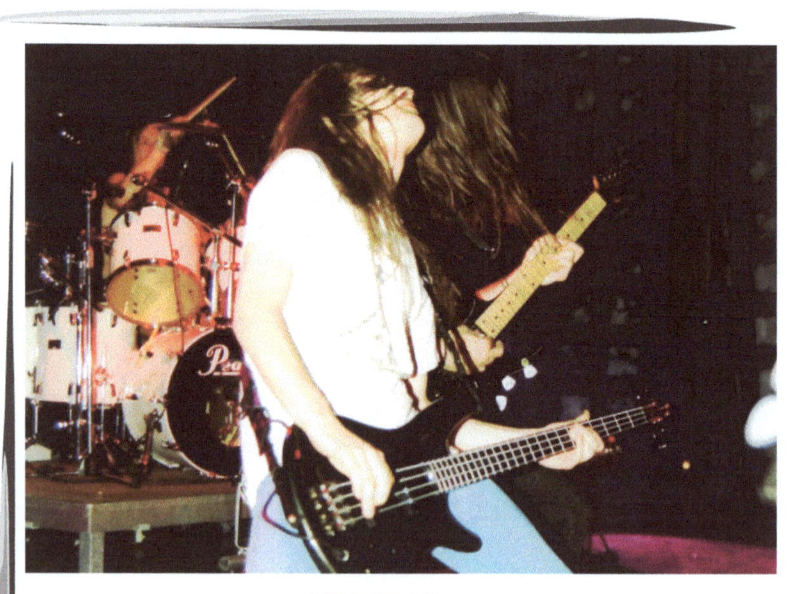

KREATOR 1990

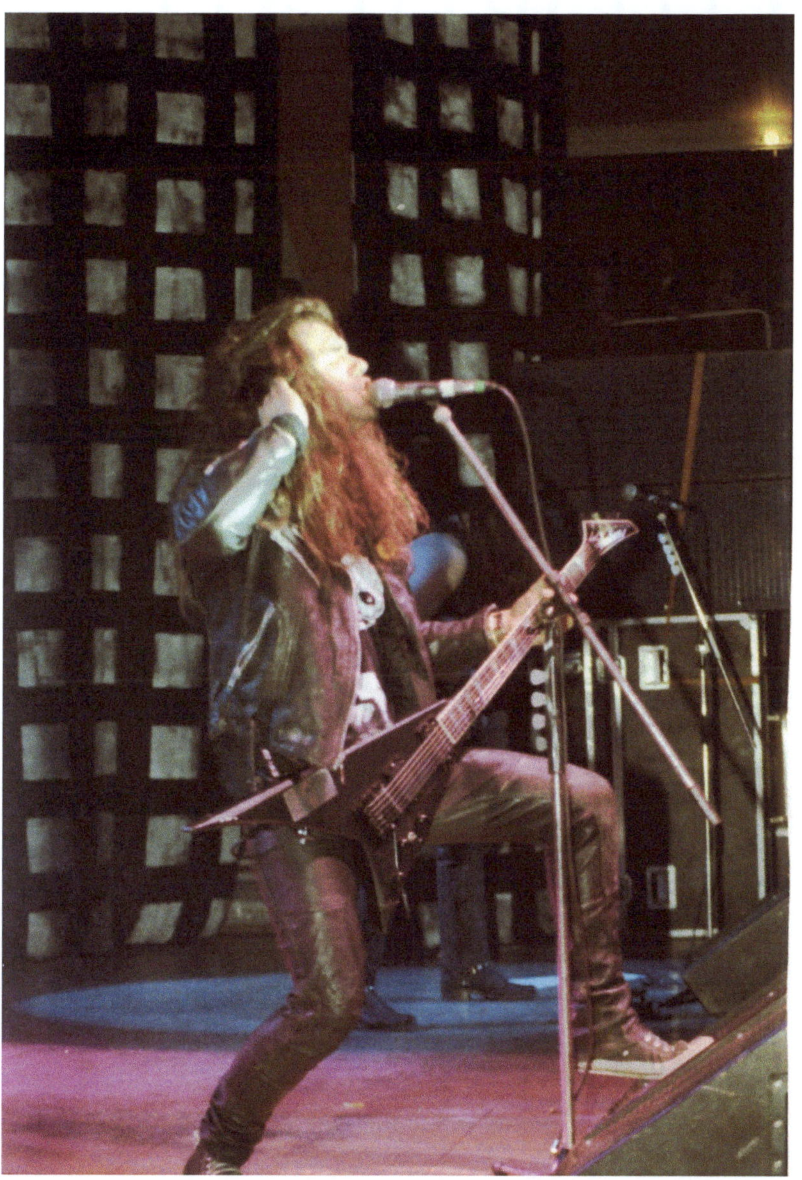

MILLE PETROZZA 1990

MOTÖRHEAD

...and escaping Animal Taylor

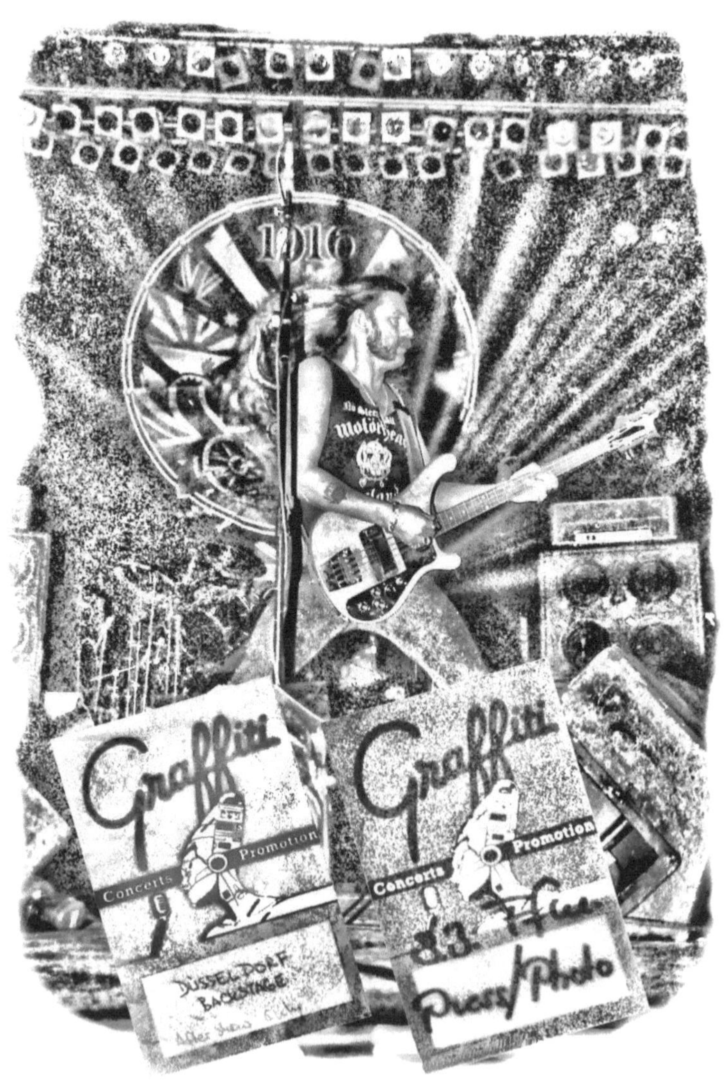

I still had the last adventure from my journey into the world of the big stars in my bones, remembering my personal disaster around the CLASH OF THE TITANS-Festival, when Sascha called me all of a sudden. "Hey Holli, we have an interview, guess who it is"? I wasn't really in the mood for that kind of question game and just said: "No clue".

"Hold on to your panties, it's MOTÖRHEAD!"

"Yeah, yeah, for sure!", that's what I thought loud. Sascha instead forgot to breathe, he was that excited. I was also close to hyperventilating but the recent disappointment prevented me from doing so. But you never learn out. So we made sure we have a car for the show, if there is need of stashing things securely.

I also had a ticket for the concert, just to make double sure. Not that I never had seen MOTÖRHEAD before, au contraire:

8.23.1981
4th SUMMERNIGHT FESTIVAL in Darmstadt at the stadium at the Böllernfalltor including IRON MAIDEN, FOREIGNER, KANSAS, BLUE ÖYSTER CULT, 38 SPECIAL, TANK, and BLACKFOOT

12.9.1981
NO SLEEP TIL CHRISTMAS TOUR at the Phillipshalle in Düsseldorf featuring TANK

11.1.1982
IRON FIST TOUR in Düsseldorf at the Phillipshalle featuring KILLER

12.27.1984

CHRISTMAS METAL MEETING at the Pink Palace in Essen featuring MERCYFUL FATE, TALON, GIRLSCHOOL, HELIX

3.30.1986

EASTER METAL BLAST at Westfalenhalle Dortmund featuring MANOWAR, EXCITER, LAAZ ROCKIT

12.28.1988

NO SLEEP TIL 89 in Düsseldorf at the Phillipshalle featuring DESTRUCTION, CANDLE MASS, and CORONER

Topping the photo pass, Sascha even had an appointment for an interview. I had to admit that I was soooo close to freaking out. My long time faves and heroes in front of my lenses, oh man...But...I really tried to stay cool. I didn't want to experience the utter disappointment, if something went wrong, again. So I always thought this would never ever happen.

That evening at the Phillipshalle, Sascha greeted me with a hearty "Come on, let's do it." He couldn't hide his own disbelief though. So he went to the ticket-counter with his best "You won't get rid of me face."

"We have an interview along with a photo pass, it's for Sascha and Holli, can you check please?" Busy-looking, the lady plowed through piles of envelopes and sheets, and she plowed and plowed and plowed.

And then, finally…"Ah, here they are."

So what? Did she really just say that? Can't be true. Sascha held on to the envelopes so tight as if the devil was following him. So I made it fast-paced into a silent corner at the overcrowded parking lot. He tore the envelope open and his eyes began to gleam. "It worked, God damnit, yeahhhhhh."

So I quickly sold the ticked I had bought as a safety measure, making one fan very happy and away we go into the crowds…hmmmm, okay, we walked through the press-entry within a short time and dressed up with our backstage tickets we were somewhat important all of a sudden.

We noticed all the hundreds of eyes, staring at our leather jackets, aiming at the adhesive patches we now had on them. It felt great and we caught ourselves from time to time with a swollen chest, heads held high, presenting our major win. But we didn't just come to party, we had to work to do. So we went to the stage and at the side of the stage there was the magic entry, guarded by our friends, the friendly bouncers. Back in the 80's most of these guys came from bike-clubs and they were a pretty rough bunch.

Due to their profession they let us pass with a grim look on their faces, giving us the feeling to be uninvited. And then this feeling of pure amazement overcame me. I've never been behind the stage at this place. After all these countless shows I saw at this place, I was finally there where only the stars and their crews had access.

Woaaahhhhhhh!!!!!!!!!!!!!!!!!!!!!!!!

Behind the first door the darkness surrounding us ended and the home of the rockstars started to shine at us. A quick glance through the periphery of the backstage-area and all persons had been scanned and sorted out into known and unknown. Sascha asked his way to the promoter and faced a beautiful young lady in the end. I couldn't hear what they were talking about, it as quite noisy there, but then Sascha waved me to him.

"We have an interview with MOTÖRHEAD, I'm freaking out." And he whispered into my ear "With Phil Campbell."

This time there was no trace of him disliking his interview-partner as we had it with MEGADETH recently. We followed the instructions of the promoter without a moan into one of the dressing rooms, where the undoubted number one logo in the metal world was visible on the door: Snaggletooth, the MOTÖRHEAD-LOGO!!!!!!!!!!!!!!!!!!!!!!!

So the old fashioned recording device was quickly positioned on the table, inspected for its functionality of course, all questions written down on a small paper sheet and the excitement under control...Tadaaaaaa!!!!!!!!!!!!!

A really cheerful Phil Campbell entered the small and scarcely clad room. Sascha and inferior me were completely unaware of what Phil would donate more than 45 minutes of his precious time for us, being extremely talkative. His first move was a six-pack of beer on the table. You didn't have to ask us twice and we made sure the cans would be emptied in a jiffy.

Sascha was in his element. It felt kind of frightening to see and experience how a ten years younger guy could actually talk me into the ground with his vast knowledge of the English language. From question to question I felt that certain pressure underneath my belly, asking for relief, but there was not a really good moment on the horizon for a break.

I absolutely did not want to miss a second or a single word of this meeting and I had the piss swimming in my eyes already, when I finally asked Phil about the locations of the loo. He was not really sure about it and pointed me towards the right side, towards the dressing rooms of the stars, where the toilet for the upper class was supposed to be.

I only had that toilet symbol in my eyes when I hastily entered the room, but it was not the sign that was waiting for me, instead I faced a grim-looking Philthy "Animal" Taylor, the MOTÖRHEAD - drummer. He was facing the mirror and tried to get in control of his hair. My only thought tat that moment was: "Now you will see the IRON FIST, staring in your face."

It was obvious that I had to explain myself ASAP, excusing my sudden intrusion. Within a break of a second I spoke some of the few words I knew in English: "Sorry, the toilet?"

With a fitting animal-like gesture his hand, including his

pointing finger, swung towards the exit. "On the right side, man." It thundered through my ears. I only wanted to get rid of my load and was far away from further disturbing him, so I immediately swung around and yelled a "Sorry Mr. Taylor: "He quickly followed me and slammed the door shut right behind my back, which gave me some unwanted tailwind, helping my to find my place of relief finally.

That short experience felt like an eternity for me, but it was all in all only three minutes which had passed since I had left the interview room. So I noticed that nobody had really missed me and Sascha and Phil were chatting and chatting, until...

...the promoter showed up and made it quite clear that it was over now. It was time for the photo-shooting which was on schedule and took place in the room next to us. It was press only, oh, and yes, I was press!

Phil gave us a hearty "Thank you" for the good time we had and invited us to the next show coming up in Frankfurt at the Kongresshalle including a photo pass, of course.

So what went on today? My pulse rose. Is it Christmas time today? We accepted the offer gladly, even though we did not know at that time how we should make it here. Phil instructed the promoter and she ok'ed things.
In the room next to us the other colleagues from the press were gathering in front of a white screen. And the he entered the room. LEMMY!

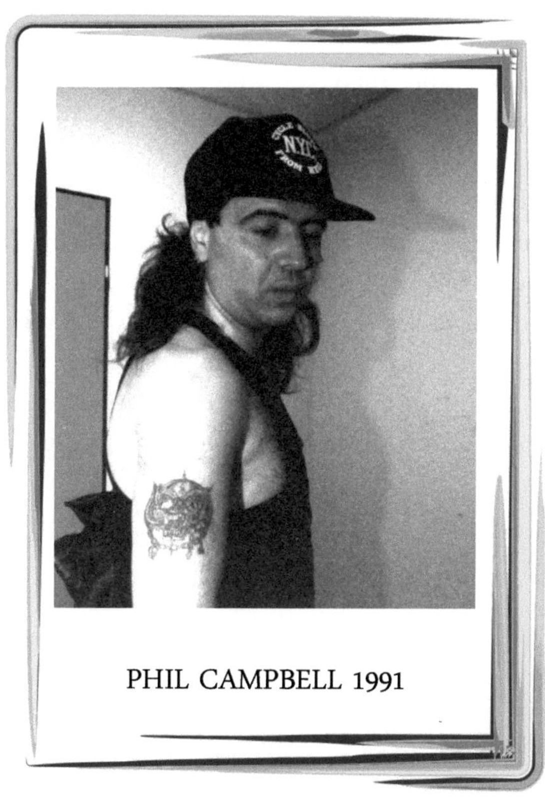

PHIL CAMPBELL 1991

You don't stand too often in front of your idol, especially such a great! I was a bit baffled when I found out that I had to lower my head in order to see his face though. I am roughly 6 and a half tall...quite amazing indeed.

Nevertheless, this was quite an amazing experience to be here right now. Mr. Taylor had already calmed down and the other guys were in a good mood too.

Everything went down really fast, five minutes for a few pics with the band and then we were complimented out of the room. Okay, the band had to prepare for the show, of course.

We missed the opening act that night, which didn't really faze us. The best thing for me, as a rookie photographer, was yet to come. with my pass I was allowed to enter a place, which I only entered in my wildest dreams, the photographer's pit.

This thing was huge and tons of security guys were waiting for some action, catching the flying fans and bring them outside again.

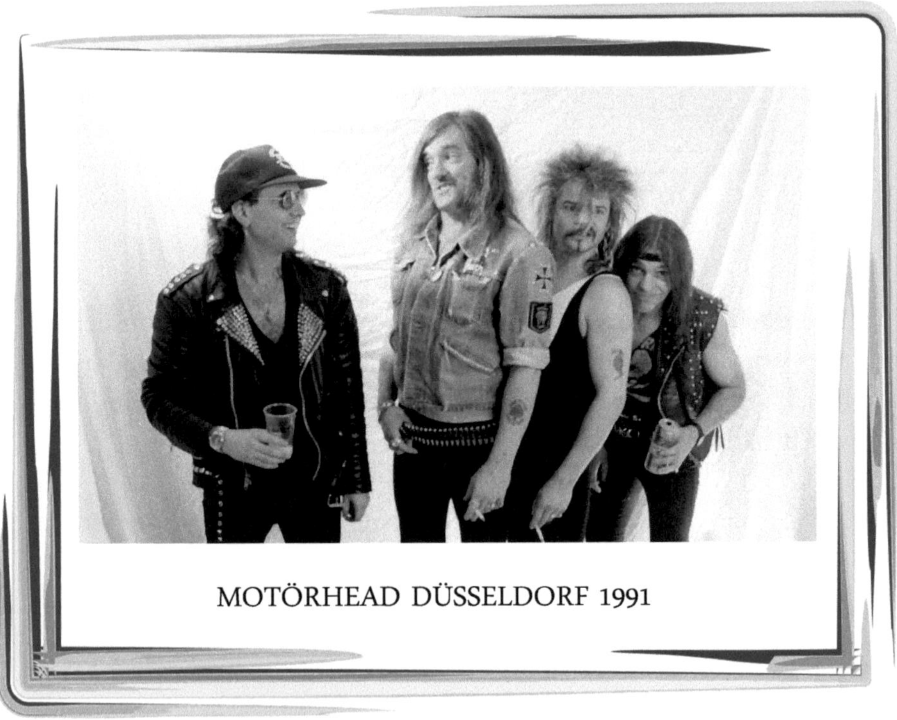

MOTÖRHEAD DÜSSELDORF 1991

The lights went out and the towering bass-cubes thundered, competing against each other and MOTÖRHEAD did another great show after their obligatory "WE ARE MOTÖRHEAD, AND WE PLAY ROCK'N ROLL." On command the dreadful-looking security guys let us enter the pit.

In a time where you had a maximum of 36 pics on your film roll, no flash allowed, with only three songs time to shoot, you could get frustrated really quick. So you finally make it to such a place and you don't have enough cash to buy a couple of rolls.

The fear of fucking up the pics drove me nuts during the gig, so there goes out the hooray to the modern digital world, combined with the possibility of immediate control at the place of your shootings.

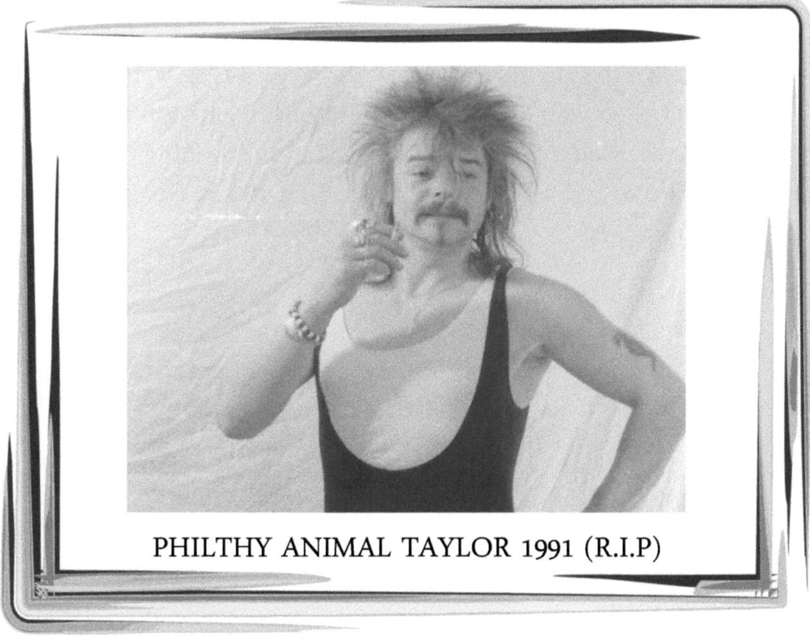

PHILTHY ANIMAL TAYLOR 1991 (R.I.P)

After the most bitter end of the third songs the rented security-hulklings drove us out of the pit and back to the rest of the crowd of fans, roughly 5,000 on that day. I was a shy young boy at that time, but I knew that some folks took shots from out of the crowd, far away from the reach of the security guys, but then I also saw how rough some got handled by the security, when they got caught taking pics. So we ended up enjoying the concert. With a humming sound in my ears the best day of my life so far ended and I only prayed that the pics turned out good.

After a short wait I was assured that my pics came out ok for my equipment and my limited abilities and I knew my next chance was Frankfurt, so it was my mum who had to suffer, borrowing me some money, so that I could buy some high resolution films, which allowed to take shots in the dark without using a flash. Well, they actually should do that, ten deutschmarks for one roll, cough, cough...

The few days of wait passed away pretty fast and off we went with a borrowed car from my friend, heading towards Frankfurt in an old VW Jetta. Thank God it was Saturday and we could go early.

The traffic jams, we were so afraid of, didn't happen and so we made it way too early to the show. The place was deserted and right next to the fairgrounds, where we were at, we had those huge buildings towering into the sky. I had never seen those in my life before, we were in the banking district and looking all the way up from below made me feel dizzy and I almost fell over, but I was still sober.

So we had enough time to stroll around being super hungry and looking for a fast food place. Somehow the skyscraper district did not seem to come to an end, trying to find something to eat here seemed to be impossible. So we marched on an on when we finally saw the sign leading to the mail railway station. There should be something for sure. So we walk through that building attracting the attention of two police officers, who also felt attracted by our looks.

"Can we see your tickets?"

"Nope, we only wan..."

We didn't finish the sentence, when the grim looking officer told us to leave the building ASAP, since we had no tickets. We had to leave immediately.

So we ended up on the street again without any food in our bellies. Fuck that! We were no junkies looking for a shot. This senseless trip had cost us a lot of time, so we headed back.

A French Fries-Hut in front of the concert hall saved our lives in the end. So Sascha got busy again, looking for our gifts for the day, this time also early enough. The place got crowded really fast and today CYCLE SLUTS FROM HELL and the local matadors from TANKARD were on the bill. I still didn't know a thing about the SLUTS, since we missed them at the last show, you couldn't Google up information back then. The only thing I knew was, that Ex-OVERKILL guitarist Bobby Gustafson would play there.
Somehow Sascha did not come back and I had this shitty feeling creeping up my neck that we might have made the journey in vain.150 miles for nothing, maybe they just took us off the list?

But there he was, snaking elegantly through the crowds, coming up and he did not look as if he had just eaten spiders. "It was quite a battle again, as you can imagine, but I found the boss, you know how I am.

Here are the tickets." The evening was safe now.

The Festhalle had already filled up with a few thousand fans, when we finally made it inside, joining the masses to see TANKARD who were already playing a hometown gig. The first three songs were already over and it was only two more pics for me. Then some beer into the gaping void and a short inspection of the merchandise booth to see all the goodies on display.

During the break Sascha spotted Phil Campbell in the backstage area and made sure he got noticed by him. He came to the fence and said hello to us. But after only two short sentences of smalltalk his guys called him back into the backstage zone. Well,that's life, light's out and start to work now!

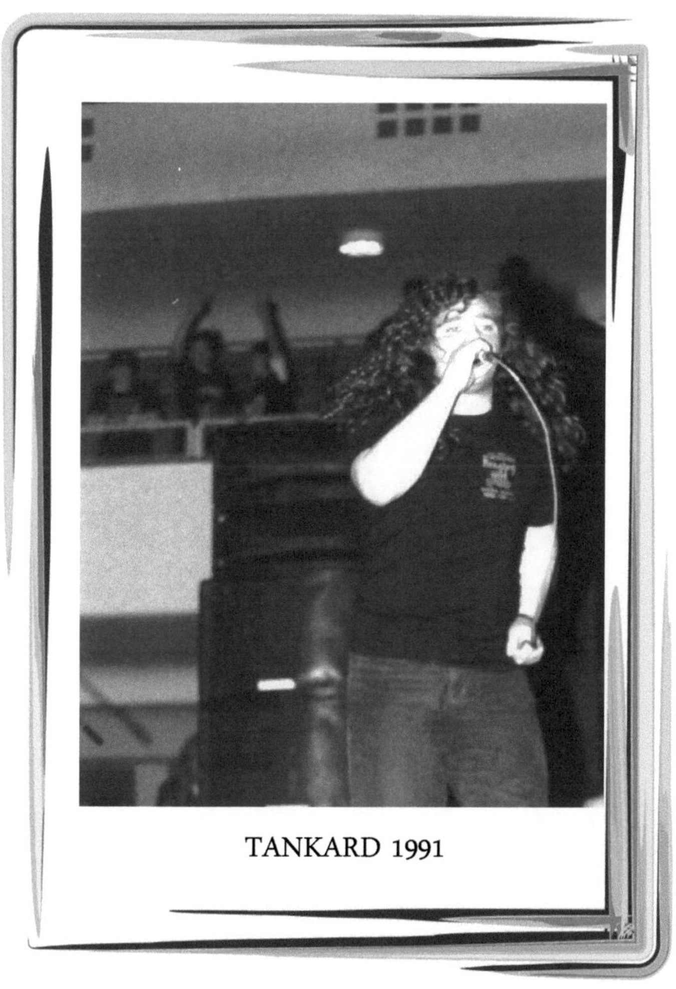

TANKARD 1991

CYCLE SLUTS FROM HELL-and me in the pit. I had never seen that kind of a band before in my life.

A metal band with a female vocalist, no, not only one but four of them. Four bicycle sluts from hell on stage. They lived up to their name for sure. My camera went into the red-hot mode and the crowd seemed to be in awe by the sights. OVERKILL lost their guitarist at that time and the girls grabbed Bobby Gustavson to join them. He seemed to be quite happy with his fate.

How much fun is involved in working was an experience we made that day. Right before the MOTÖRHEAD 1916 "Lights out over Europe"-Tour show entered the stage Sascha grabbed

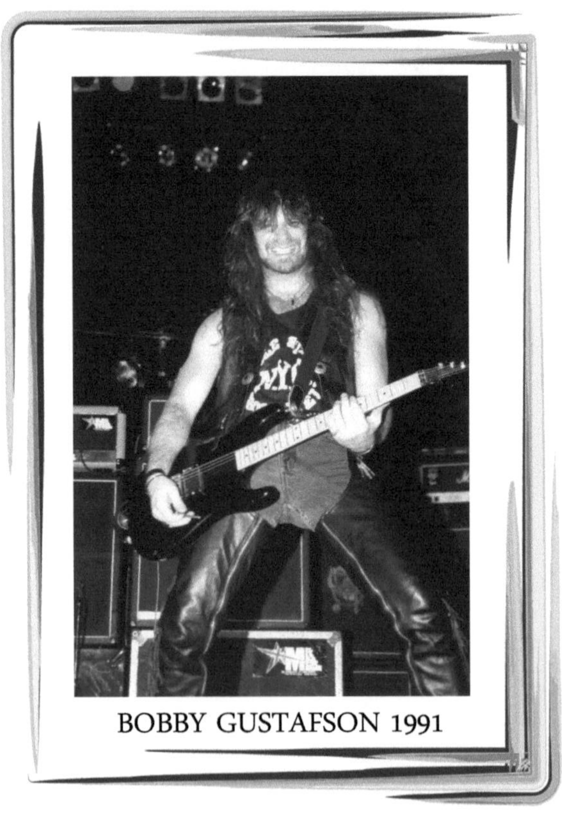

BOBBY GUSTAFSON 1991

a bit more work to bring home. An interview with the girls from the band brought him and his typewriter a long evening at home. Being so impressed by the view and the band I decided to head to the merchandise booth and buy a baseball cap.

This cap was with with me for a lot of years until it literally fell apart on my head. With the car I borrowed from my friend, we had the chance to see this concert, but there were also obligations coming along. No alcohol. Lemmy and Co. were in the mood to party after the gig and we made it to the old town of Frankfurt to a pub called SPEAK EASY. So I see my self there, not being allowed to drink a bit, the car had to be back the next morning, what a nightmare for me.

So we headed into that hessian metal-pit with the whole road crew and even without some gasoline the whole eveing was an unforgettable experience for life. I later found out that MÖTORHEAD had already played the decent amount of more than a hundred gigs that year, just to promote their album "1916". This sounds like a pretty tough job, but well, It's fun. I, for myself, needed at least ten years in my career as a musician to reach that number.

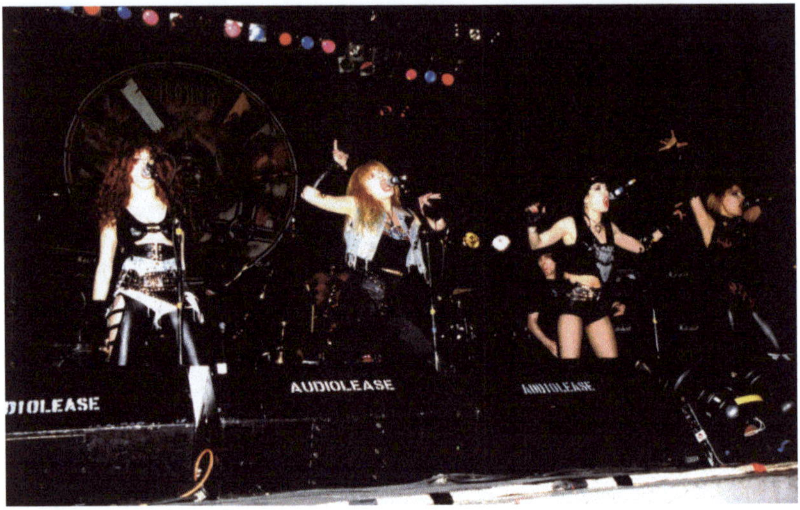

CYCLE SLUTS FROM HELL 1991

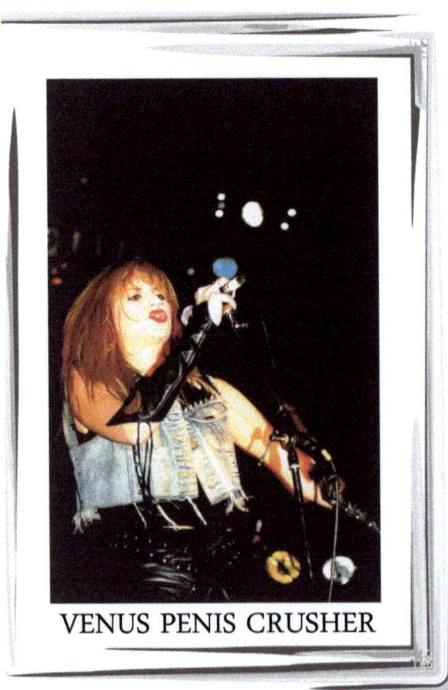

VENUS PENIS CRUSHER

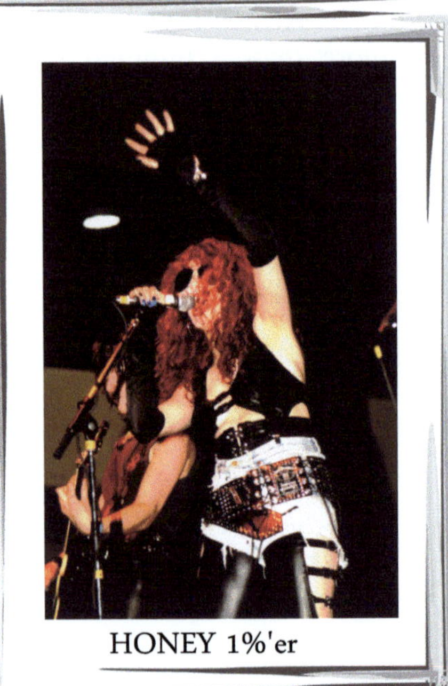

HONEY 1%'er

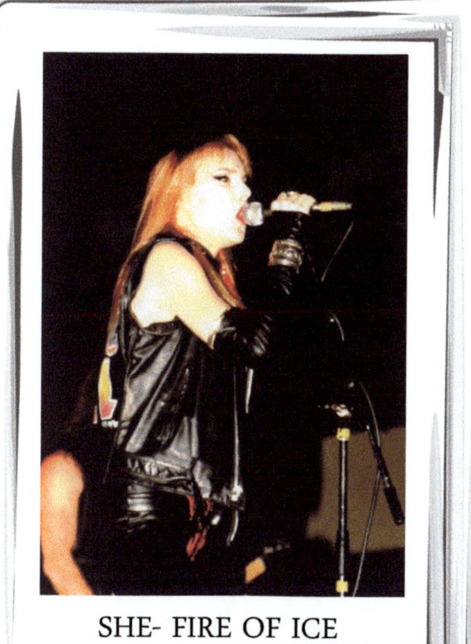

SHE- FIRE OF ICE

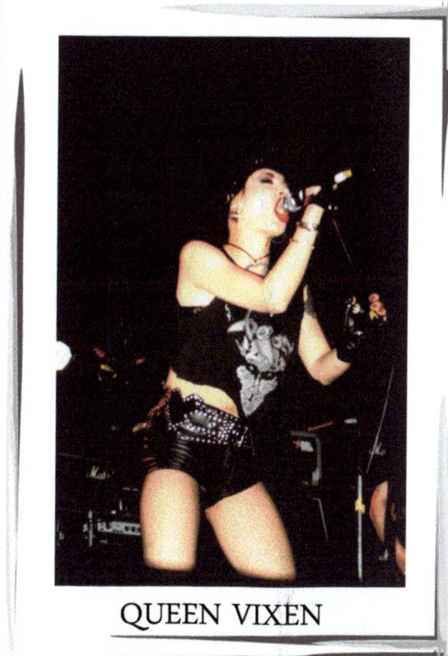

QUEEN VIXEN

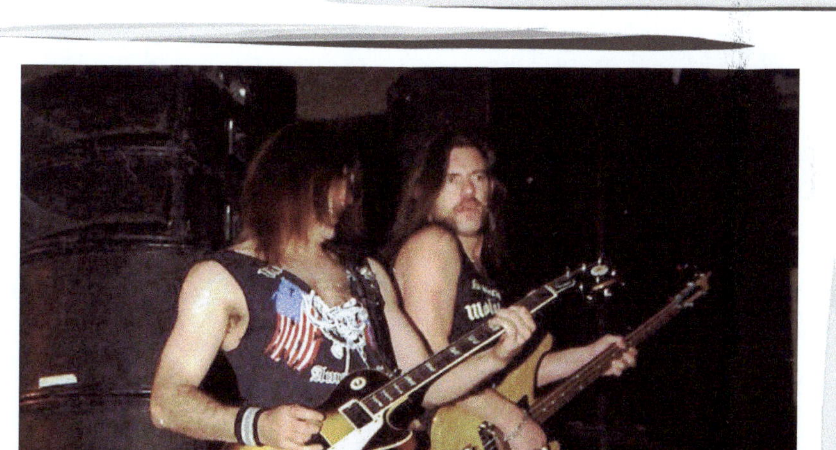

WURZEL & LEMMY 1991 ((R.I.P))

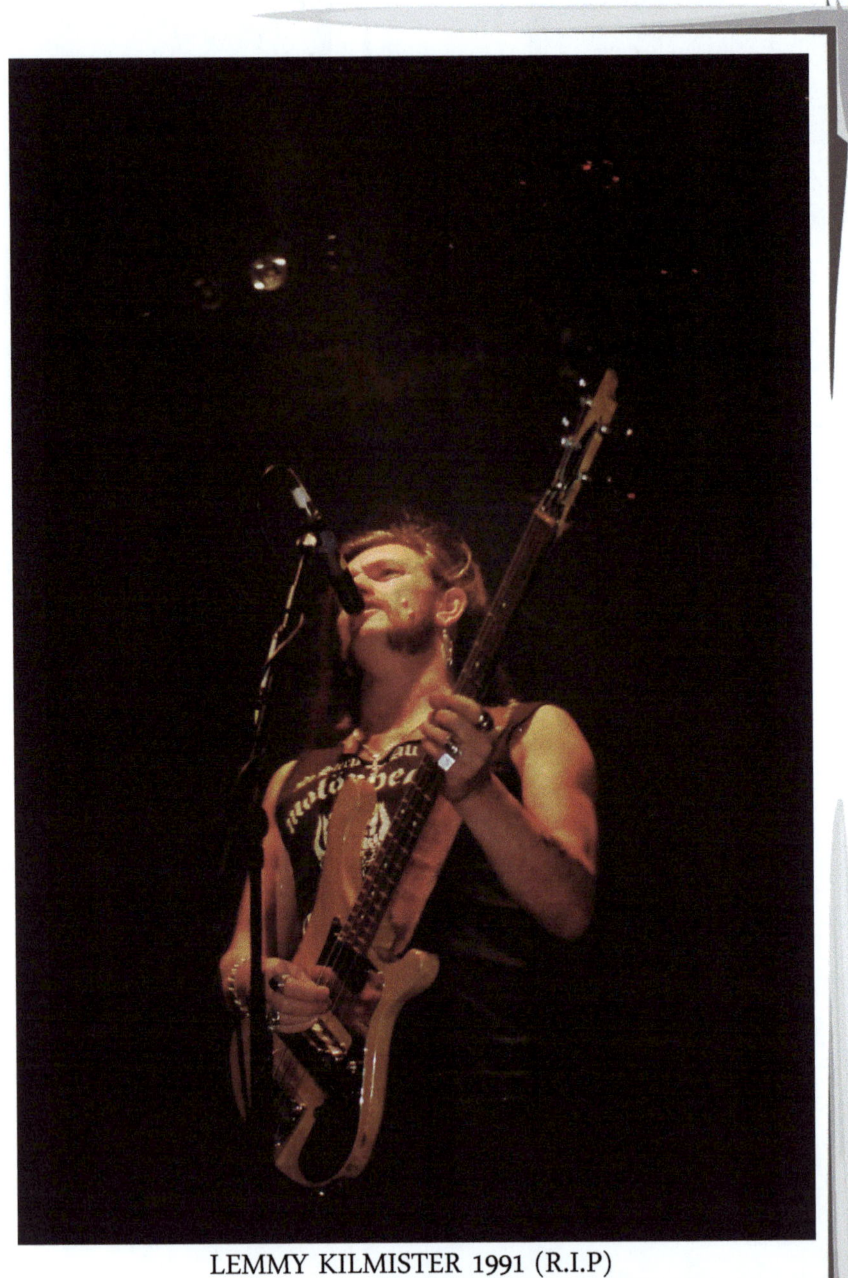

LEMMY KILMISTER 1991 (R.I.P)

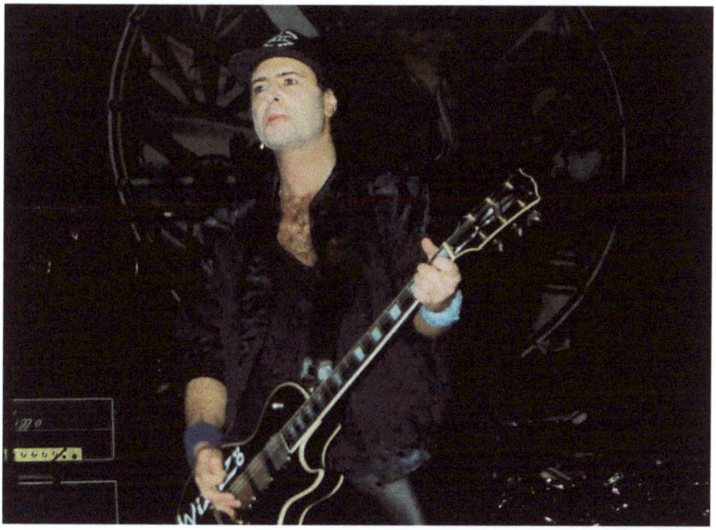

PHIL CAMPBELL 1991

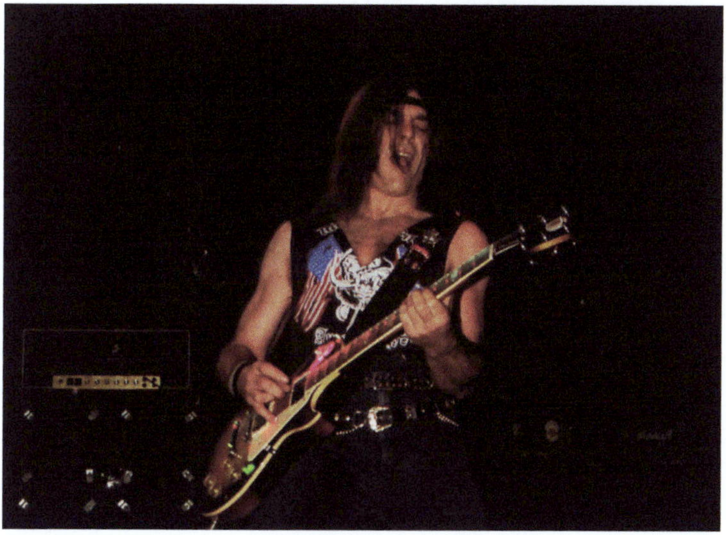

WURZEL 1991 (R.I.P)

JUDAS PRIEST

The Priest is back!

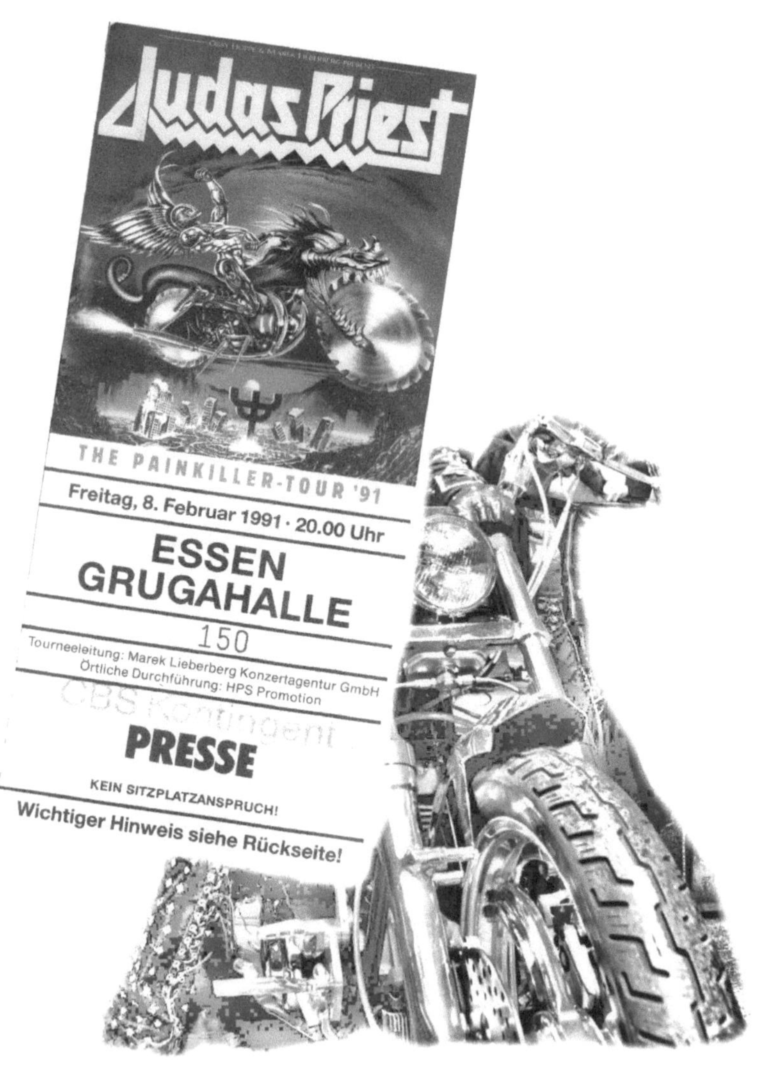

This star-spangled line up at the Painkiller-Tour was reason enough, even without photo permit and interview dates, to drive to Essen to the Grugahalle.

At least I got in for free, which is also something, right? JUDAS PRIEST had this tremendous record done after an insane court trial where some parents opened a case, since their kids had committed suicide. right next to them, the police found an album by the band on the turntables, which led to the aforementioned case.

"Beyond the realms of death" was almost a speel of death for the band, since the offending party insisted of having heard satanic instructions on the record when played backwards. BULLSHIT!!!!! With that farce on their mid they went out and created an absolute masterpiece. The other two bands joining that evening put the stamp of excellence on the concert bill. ANNIHILATOR were opening and the up-and coming skyrocketing guys from PANTERA gave the debut in Germany.

"The Priest is back." Rob Halford saying this, left an incredible effect on that evening. The show: absolutely an amazing hammer for eternity.

MEGADETH

Allowance for Alice in Chains...

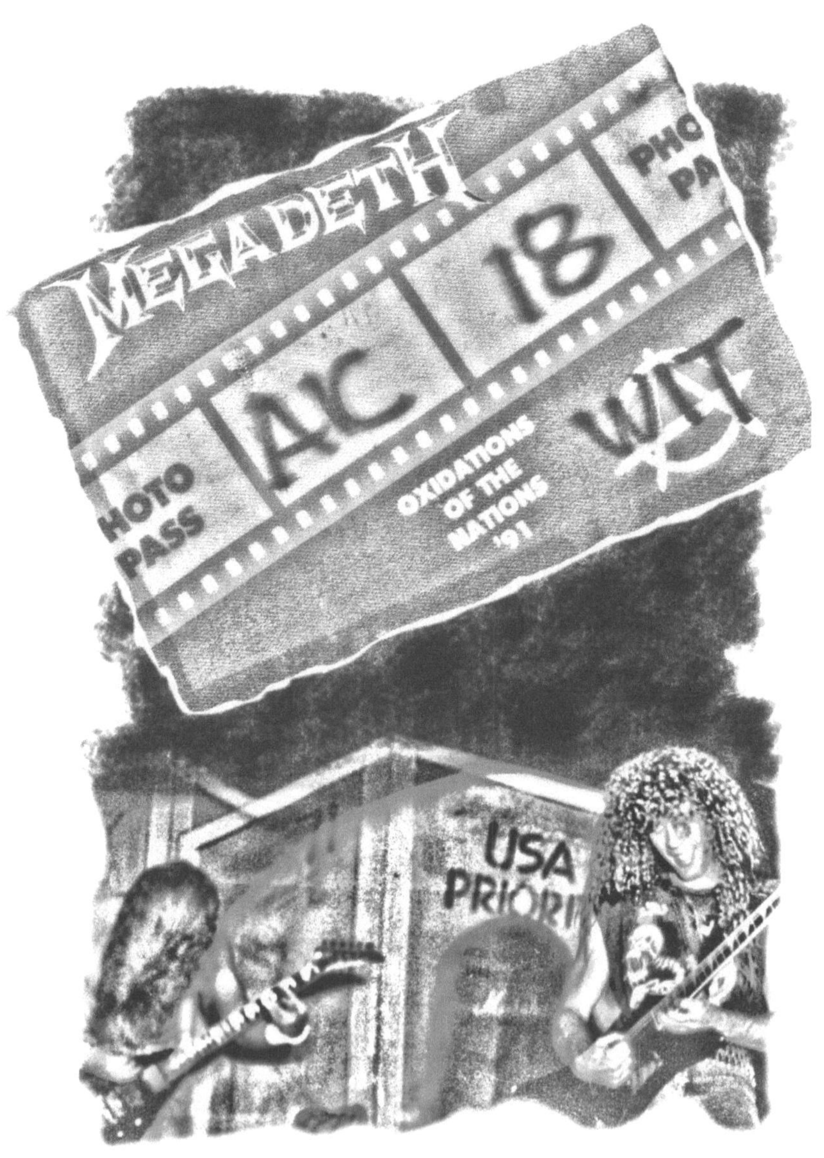

A very certain kind of stupidity for me, was the fact that you did not get the permission to shoot all bands, but only a few select. So, during a night it could happen that you only had the rights for one band but not for the other bands.

The differences had been marked on the adhesive patches with a sharpie, often almost not readable at all. So, if you got lucky, even the security guys were unable to read the scribblings on your patch in the dark. Today I was not so lucky, ALICE IN CHAINS gave their permit, THE ALMIGHTY was a pretty unsure thing and MEGADETH was an absolute no go. Well, that didn't work with me as an experienced guest and owner of a tele-objective.

So out into the crowd far away from the reach of the securities and then a few nicey nice pics of the full stage. That's how it's done. Coming with the experience you become more and more creative, when it comes to getting a few shots. You only want to promote the band, nothing more, nothing less.

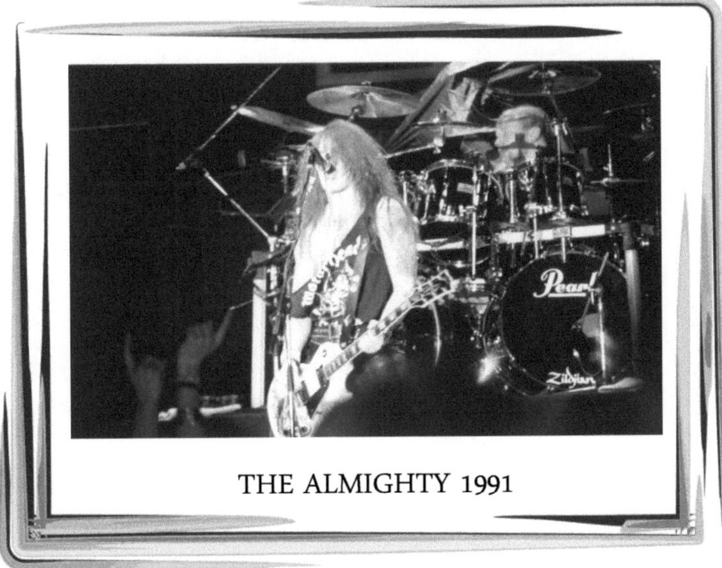

THE ALMIGHTY 1991

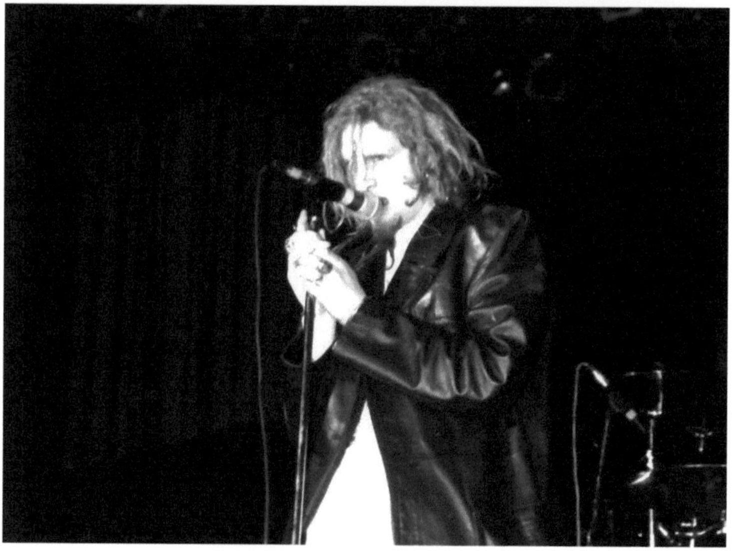

ALICE IN CHAINS 1991

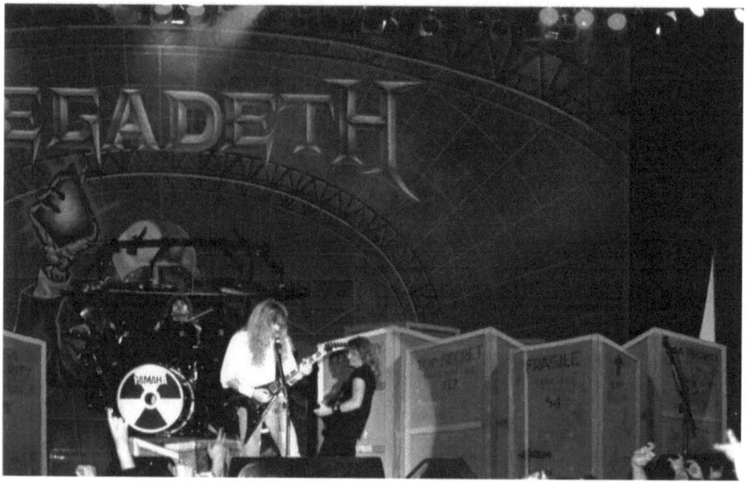

MEGADETH 1991

RUNNING WILD

and terrible Sven

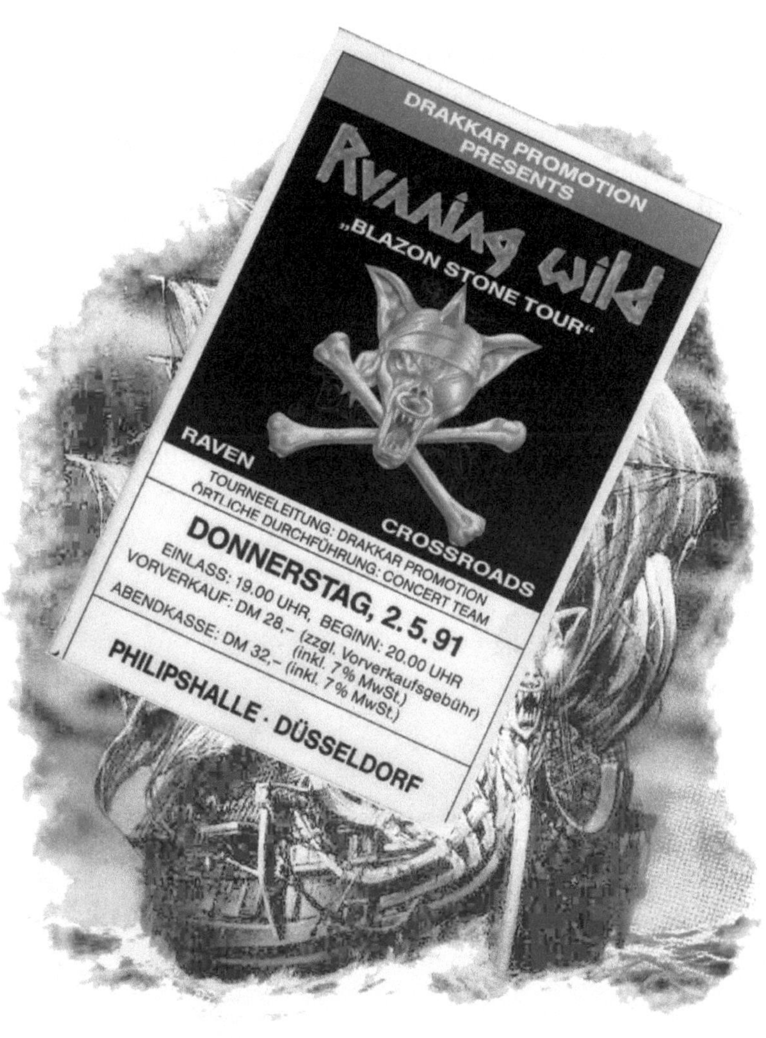

Compared to the size of venues this year was the most successful for RUNNING WILD, here in Germany.

As a headliner at the Phillipshalle, well, that was something for sure. Rock 'n Rolf and his Pirates invited a few guests and CROSSROADS and RAVEN were among those bands. CROSSROADS didn't have an easy standing as the opening act, but managed to convince the audience thus receiving some applause. The Gallagher brothers of RAVEN completely lived up to their experience and played it completely out. Completely crazy but dead on spot they presented their "Life at the Inferno"

Since the place was so big RUNNING WILD made sure to bring a fitting light show. One of the highlights next to their greatest hits show was the drum-solo by Jörg Michael. In those times when AMON AMARTH were still running around the Christmas tree with their drums the pirates hailing from Hamburg already had a Viking ship on stage. Lead by the hand of the terrible Sven it moved to the stage's end and also up in the air. In the middle the drums and their master, face in the wind.

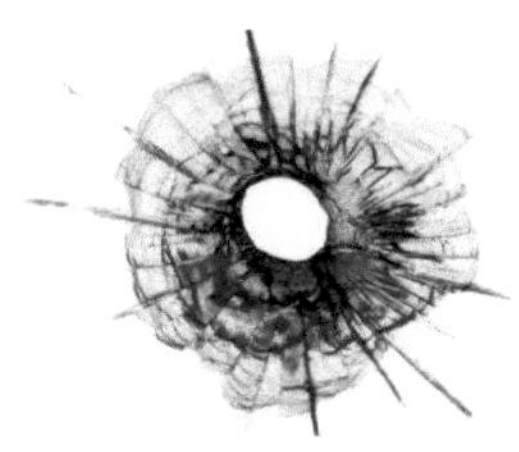

Guess I will go there,
not this on, or maybe?

Our rare staff meeting took place in Saschas room at his parent's home. This was the place to hand over your done jobs, concert-reviews, interviews and record-critics. And me, the layout-uncle took 'em all with him to feed all the info into his computer. No floppy, no e-mail, wasn't existent, nobody had that.

But there are a lot of things you do, when you want a better result. Sascha always shared the info of up and coming things to do, "who goes and who not". Arguments about this were rare, there was always something for everybody.

Sascha, who was a really smart guy, always found new ways to get advertisers into the boat, which helped our mag to grow and grow, the number of pages increased.

With the growth our efforts increased the same and we all went our own ways in the name of heavy metal. Sometimes you checked the outskirts to say so, since you wanted to have a widespread and interesting publication.

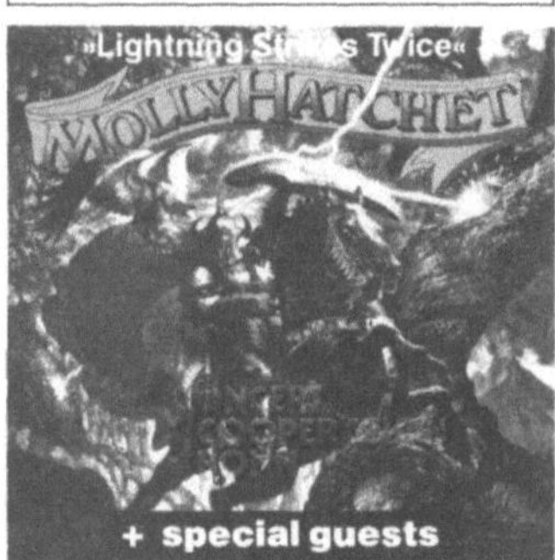
Mittwoch, 14. März 1990 · 20 Uhr
KÖLN · STADTHALLE MÜLHEIM
»Lightning Strikes Twice«
MOLLY HATCHET
+ special guests
Tourneeleitung:
Concertbüro Hänsel
Örtliche Durchführung:
Concert Cooperation Bonn GmbH
0514

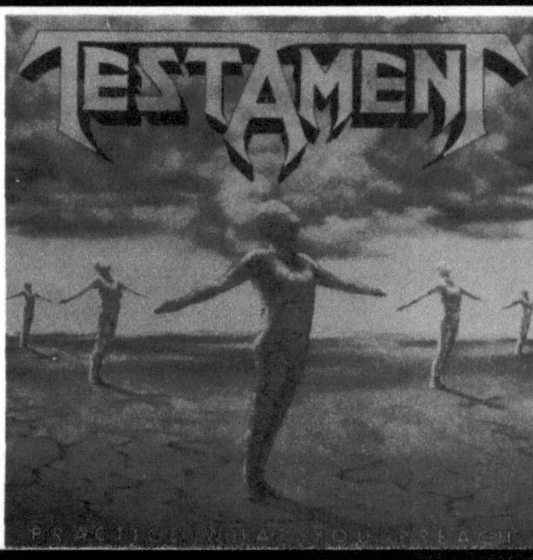
Sonntag,
21. Januar 1990
Einlaß 19 Uhr, Beginn 20 Uhr
Düsseldorf
Tor 3
Verbilligter
Vorverkauf: 23,-
zzgl. Vorverkaufsgebühr
Abendkasse: 27,-
Cooperation:
Sunrise – HPS Promotion
TELE 5
HARD N HEAVY
TESTAMENT

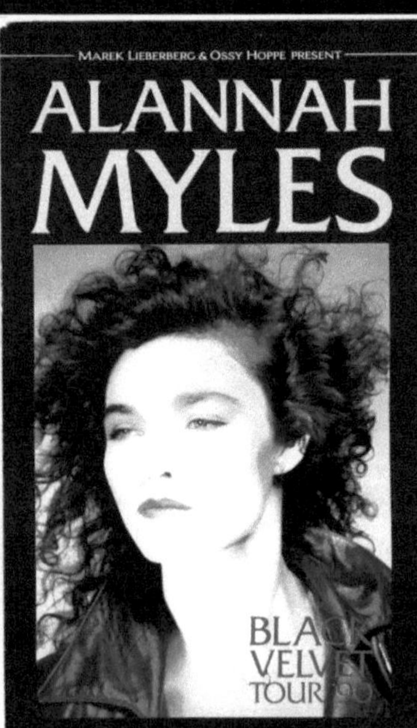
MAREK LIEBERBERG & OSSY HOPPE PRESENT
ALANNAH
MYLES
BLACK
VELVET
TOUR
Samstag, 16. Juni 1990 · 20.00 Uhr
KÖLN · LIVE MUSIC HALL
Vorverkauf: DM 25,-
zuzügl. Vorverkaufsgebühr, inkl. 7 % MwSt.
Abendkasse: DM 29,-
inkl. 7 % MwSt.
KEIN SITZPLATZANSPRUCH!
1639
Wichtiger Hinweis siehe Rückseite!

OSSY HOPPE & MAREK LIEBERBERG PRESENT
BLACK SABBATH
TOUR '90
3483
Sonntag, 21. Oktober 1990 · 20.00 Uhr · Düsseldorf · Ph
Vorverkauf: DM 33,-
zuzügl. Vorverkaufsgebühr.
inkl. 7 % MwSt.
Abendkasse: DM 38,-
inkl. 7 % MwSt.
KEIN SITZPLATZANSPRUCH!
Tourneeleitung:
Marek Lieberberg Kc
Örtliche Durchführu
HPS Promotion
WICHTIGER HINWEIS SIEHE RÜCKSEITE!

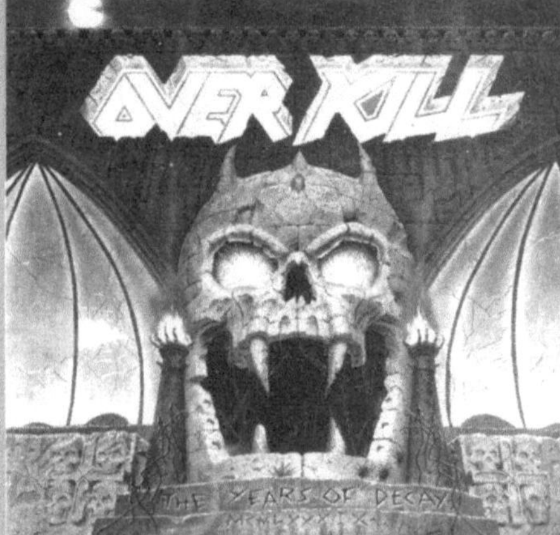
Mittwoch,
7. Februar 1990
Einlaß 19 Uhr, Beginn 20 Uhr
Düsseldorf
Tor 3
Verbilligter
Vorverkauf: 23,-
zzgl. Vorverkaufsgebühr
Abendkasse: 27,-
Cooperation:
Sunrise – HPS Promotion
TELE 5
HARD N' HEAVY
OVER KILL
THE YEARS OF DECAY

Sonntag, 1. April 1990 · 20 Uhr
DÜSSELDORF · PHILIPSHALLE

»Fire over Europe 90«

YNGWIE MALMSTEEN

+ special guest
support: China

Tourneeleitung:
Moderne Welt GmbH
Örtliche Durchführung:
Concert Cooperation Bonn GmbH

3139

Jugendliche unter 18 Jahren nur in Begleitung eines Erziehungsberechtigten. Keine Haftung für Sach- und Körperschäden. Zurücknahme der Karten nur bei Absage der Veranstaltung. Kartenpreiserstattung erfolgt nur über die Verkaufsstelle, bei der die Karte gekauft wurde, bis zwei Wochen nach Konzertdatum. Bei Verlassen der Halle verliert die Karte ihre Gültigkeit. Das Mitbringen von Glasbehältern, Dosen, Tonbandgeräten, Film- u. Videokameras, pyrotechnischen Gegenständen, Fackeln sowie Waffen ist untersagt. Bei Nichtbeachtung erfolgt Verweis aus der Halle. Ton-, Film- u. Videoaufnahmen, auch für den privaten Gebrauch, sind nicht erlaubt. Mißbrauch wird strafrechtlich verfolgt. Kaufen Sie Ihre Karten nur an den bekannten Vorverkaufsstellen. Kein Sitzplatzanspruch. Gute Unterhaltung!

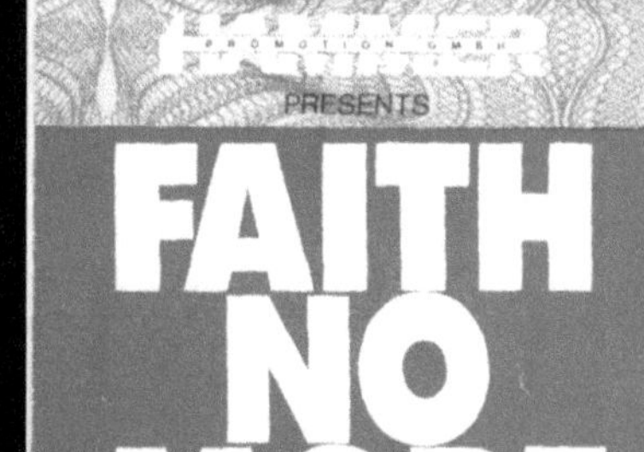

Tourneeleitung: Hammer Promotions GmbH, Frankfurt/M.
Örtliche Durchführung: Concert Team Düsseldorf

107

Keine Haftung für Sach- und Körperschaden. Zurücknahme der Karte nur bei Absage der Veranstaltung. Kartenpreiserstattung erfolgt nur über die Verkaufsstelle, bei der die Karte gekauft wurde, bis 2 Wochen nach Konzertdatum. Bei Verlassen der Halle verliert die Karte ihre Gültigkeit. Das Mitbringen von Glasbehältern, Dosen, Tonbandgeräten, Film- und Videokameras, pyrotechnischen Gegenständen, Fackeln sowie Waffen ist untersagt. Bei Nichtbeachtung erfolgt Verweis aus der Halle. Ton-, Film- und Videoaufnahmen – auch für privaten Gebrauch – sind nicht erlaubt. Mißbrauch wird strafrechtlich verfolgt. Beim Parken beachten Sie bitte die Hinweise der Ordnungskräfte. Blitzlichtfotografie nur mit Genehmigung der Tourneeleitung. Ansonsten wünschen wir einen angenehmen Abend und gute Unterhaltung.
Kein Sitzplatzanspruch

7. Mai 1990
Einlaß: 19.00 Uhr, Beginn: 20.00 Uhr
DÜSSELDORF ● TOR 3
Ronsdorfer Straße

HOT **3.** NIGHT
METAL
mit

SATYR

Tusk

THE SPOT

23.2.91, 19⁰⁰ h   Eintritt: 7,-

FRANKLINSTR. 5
JUGENDFREIZEITEINRICHTUNG

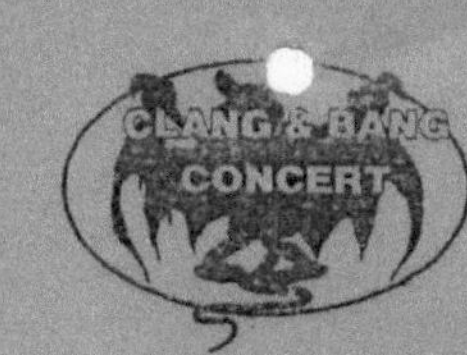

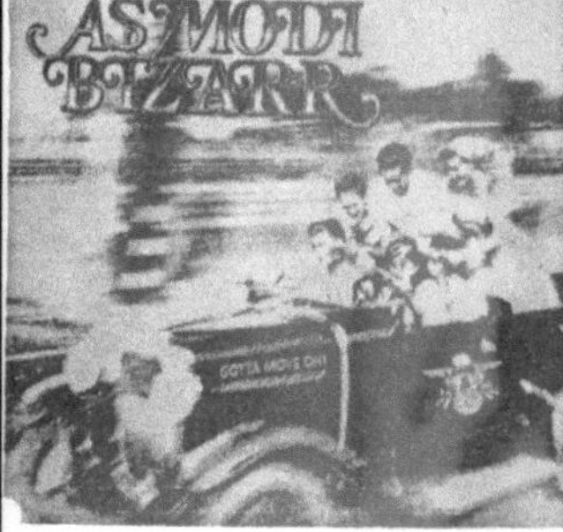

Release-Party 'n' Gig
4. 2. 1991
Beginn: 20.00 Uhr

aktionsbühne
junge **jab** Düsseldorf

Heinrich-Heine-Platz · Kasernenstraße 6

PRESSE

Jugendliche unter 18 Jahren nur in Begleitung eines Erziehungsberechtigten. Keine Haftung für Sach- und Körperschäden. Zurücknahme der Karten nur bei Absage der Veranstaltung. Kartenpreiserstattung erfolgt nur über die Verkaufsstelle, bei der die Karte gekauft wurde, bis 2 Wochen nach Konzertdatum. Bei Verlassen der Halle verliert d. Karte ihre Gültigkeit. Das Mitbringen von Glasbehältern, Dosen, Tonbandgeräten, Film- und Videokameras, pyrotechnischen Gegenständen, Fackeln sowie Waffen ist untersagt. Bei Nichtbeachtung erfolgt Verweis aus der Halle. Ton-, Film- u. Videoaufnahmen, auch für den privaten Gebrauch, sind nicht erlaubt. Mißbrauch wird strafrechtl. verfolgt. Beim Parken beachten Sie bitte die Hinweise der Ordnungskräfte. Kaufen Sie Ihre Karten nur an den bekannten Vorverkaufsstellen.

THE SISTERS OF MERCY

and other dark creatures.

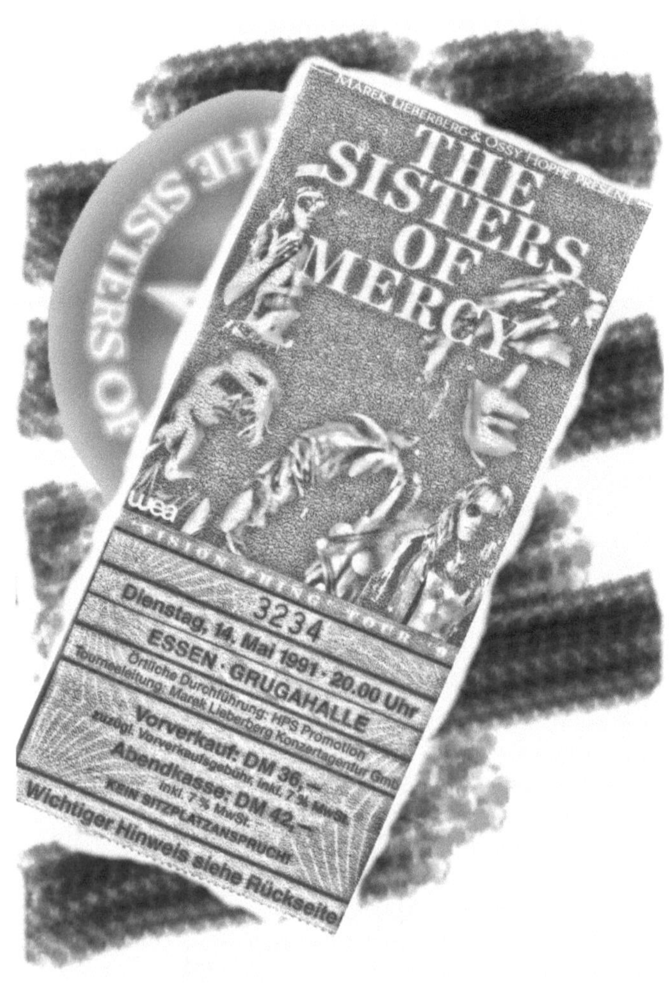

With their guitar loaded album "Vision Thing" the dark sisters not only made it into the charts but also into the hearts of a few metalheads. So this was something else. So here we go to Essen to the Grugahalle.

These days the sight of gothics is nothing uncommon anymore, back then it was a strange and uncommon sight, especially inside the venue among only a few metalheads and thousands of gothic fans. Also their way of reacting to music was different than ours. We played the air-guitar and let our heads rotate. These guys marched-in small groups-back and forth, heads looking to the ground. So, what can you say? Sometimes something new can't hurt, eh?

THE SISTERS OF MERCY, way makers of the gothic rock movement with their singer Andrew Eldritch didn't look too bad. I was missing some Wagner choirs they used on the record when they played live this was missing and this was exactly what gave the song that special flavor. Whatever, it was quite interesting and a change in the daily concert routine.

Ali Baba and the 40 thieves, or

ALICE COOPER

and the 40 dealer!

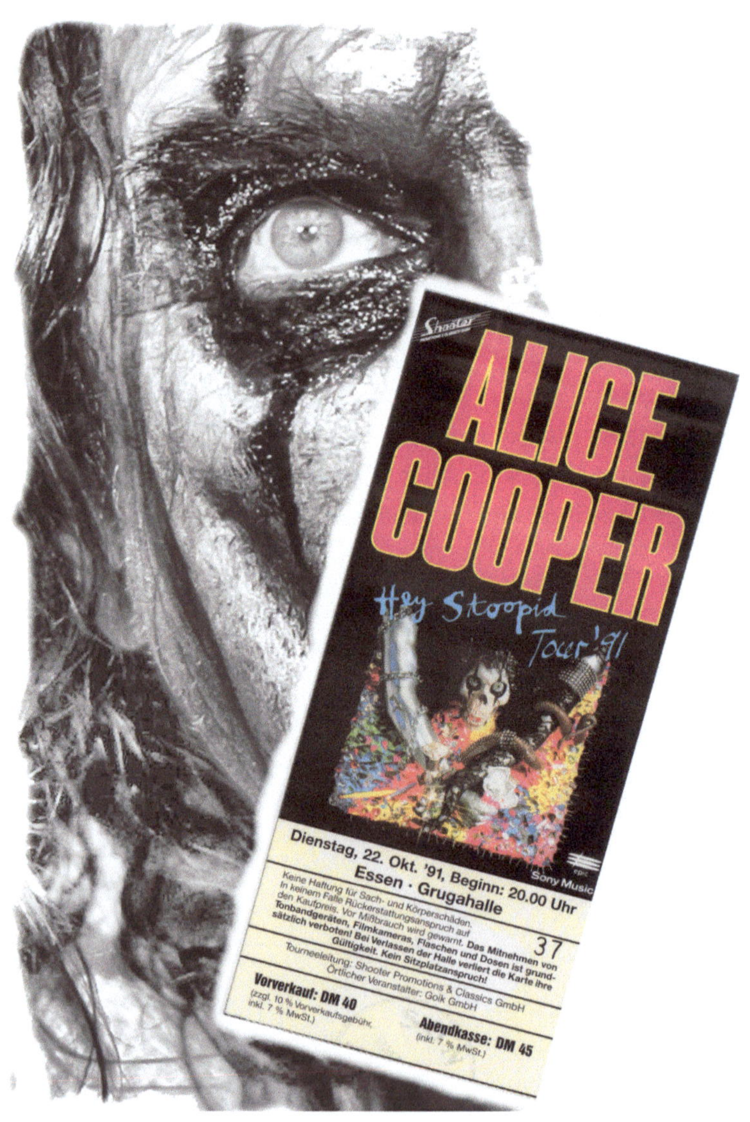

Compared to my other staff buddies incl. boss Sascha I was an old nutsack, being 27 years old. So I was the only guy to know the even older than me sack ALICE COOPER from his early days. Hmmm, not really. My older brothers was a big fan when "School's Out" had been released in the early 70's.The only thing I knew besides that hit he had was a newspaper clip from our local newspaper from wayyyy back then, where the police arrested roughly 40 drug dealers at an ALICE COOPER gig in Düsseldorf. Yep, and also a few antics from his live shows were known to me, of course.

So the best thing to do is finally see this guy after decades and go to one of his concerts. Done as said. The Grugahalle was completely sold out and almost ready to explode from the masses filling it. This surely was not linked to his seventies hit. It was "Poison", his actual smash hit in the charts, which made this possible, only for the girls...whatever...

So the grandmaster showed em all that night and it was the finest of the finest. Amazing sound, super songs and a show which was very detailed and also had an amazing choreography. Tons of blood coming from a giant nail which he had rammed into an oversized hand on stage. He then went to the border of the stage and started spraying the audience with the artificial blood up to the fifth row. Rolling heads and other cut off extremities, limbs, torsos-you name it-underlined his vision of a nightmare.

One of the best things was a huge screen on stage where they played a movie starring ALICE COPPER in the clutch of extraterrestrials and being tortured. So he escapes from the hands of those beasts and runs from the movie directly through the screen onto the stage. That was brilliantly done and looked really amazing. So I say,"Heads off" errrr" Hats off".

SEPULTURA,

HEATHEN and tons of pain!

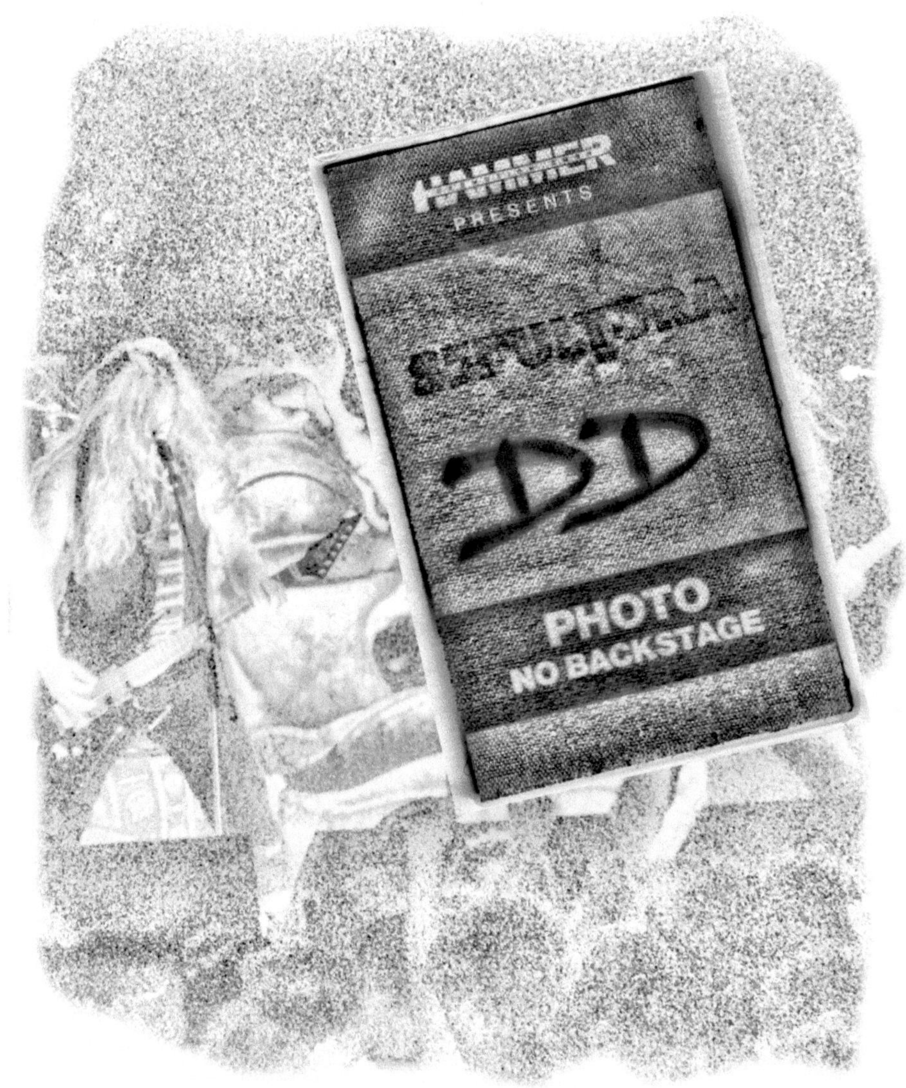

It was a known fact that SEPULTURA would go through the roof with their latest release "Arise". The TOR3 was a way to small place to cope with the onstorm of fans, who wanted to see the band.

And yes it didn't matter at all that we lived close by, didn't have to pay for tickets, just taking a few stops with the tram to come to that place. A lot of fans had to go home, since the show was completely sold out.

I knew the support band HEATHEN from their release" Breaking the Silence", another record to crown my decent collection. There was no chance for pics that night, but I managed to get the band together for an interview.

Having the honor to take pics of the Brazilian rocketeers proved to be quite a painful experience. They did not have a real pit at the TOR3. The only way to get some pics was bite, kick, push...all the way. I climbed up one of the support beams for the lightshow holding on tight to it with the left hand and taking pics-somehow-with my right hand and the heavy camera. Well, I thought just go for it, not really sure what would come out of this. The crowd was raging wild the whole gig and at the end I had tons of blue spots, a few ouches here and there and also a few decent pics.

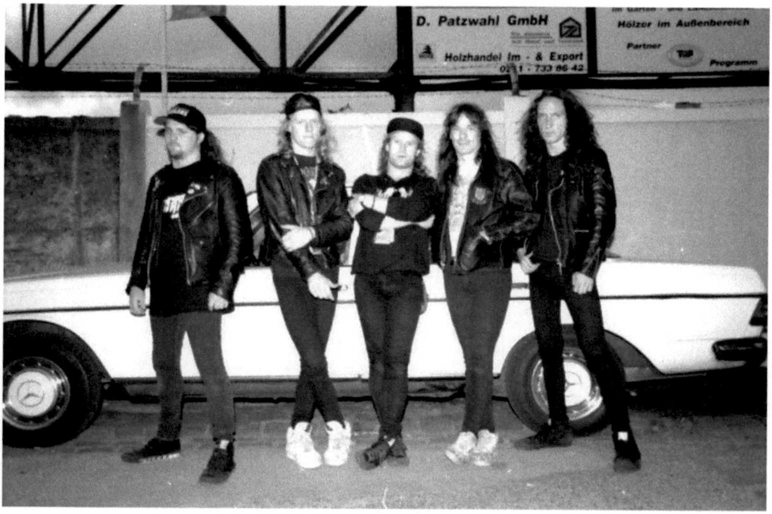

HEATHEN 1991

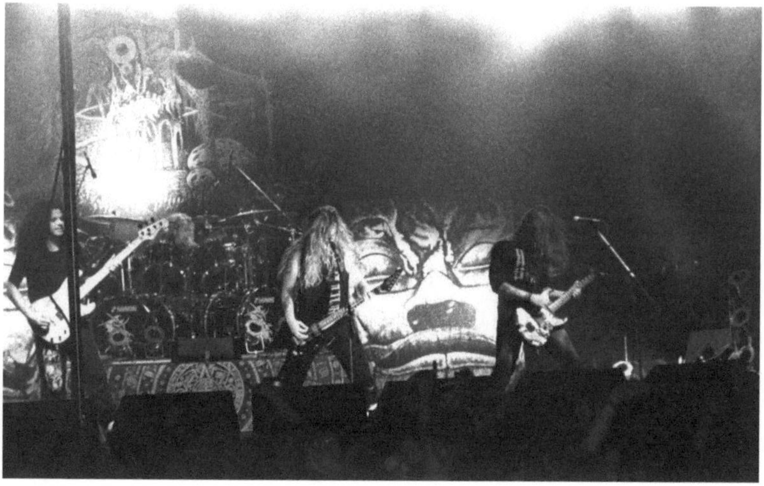

SEPULTURA 1991

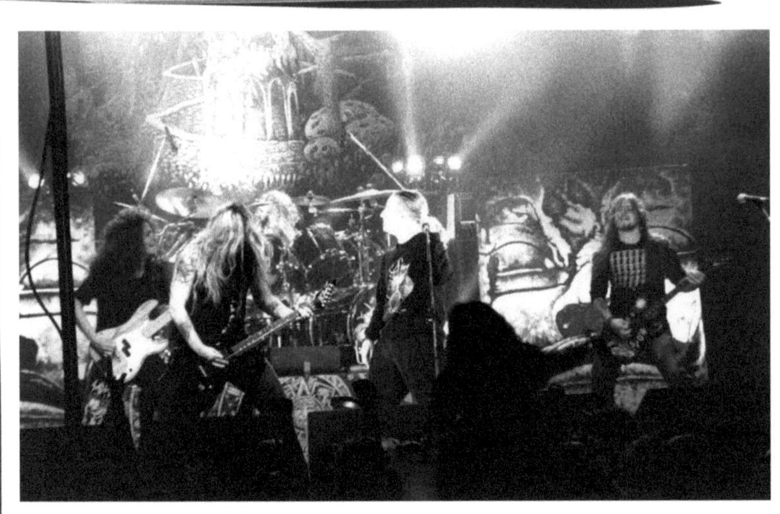

SEPULTURA 1991 (WITH PHIL RIND OF SACRED REICH)

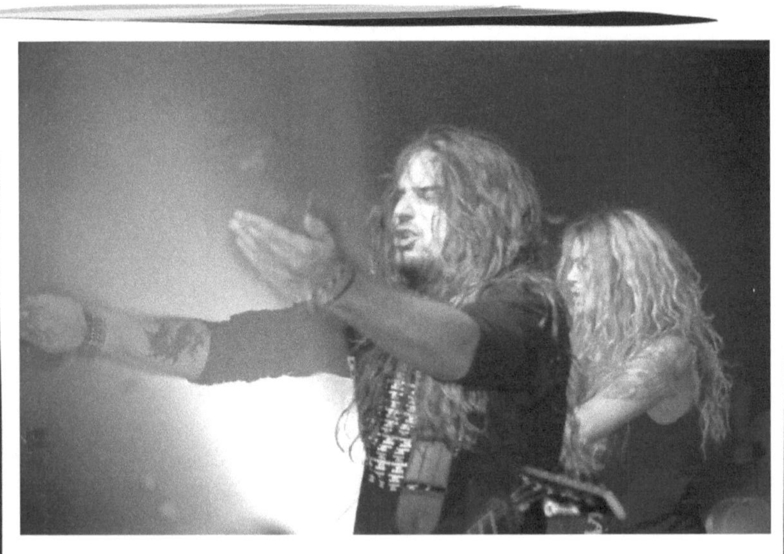

SEPULTURA 1991

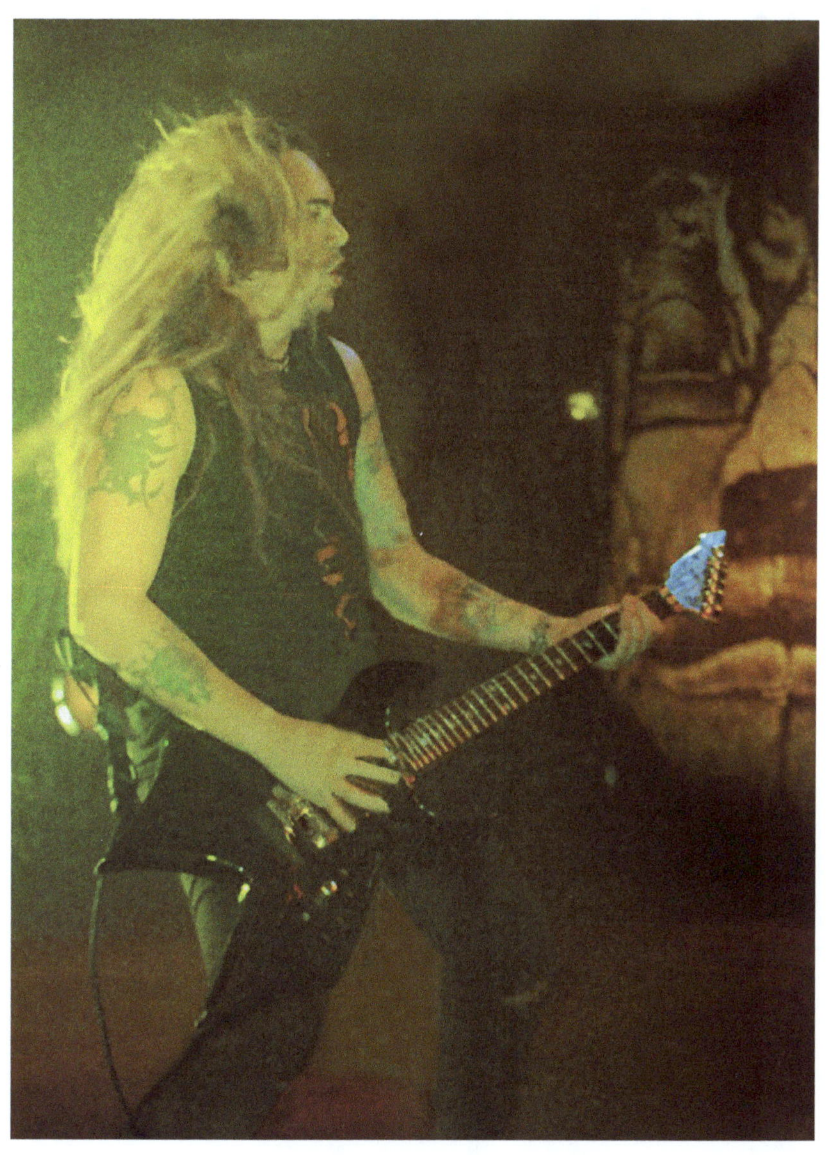

MAX CABALERA 1991

MORDRED

Rappin` Funky Time

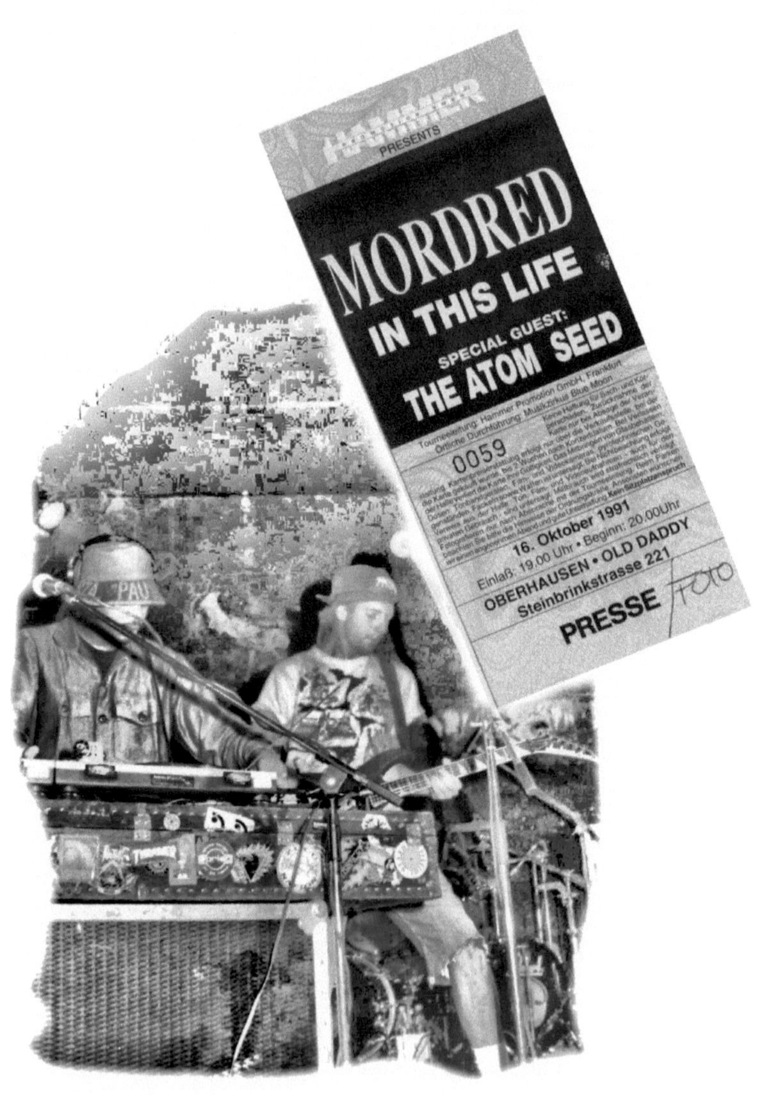

Other cities also hosted nice concerts, knowing that, Sascha rushed us into a city in the Ruhrgebiet, where you saw seldom any metal acts, the club was called Old Daddy and located in Oberhausen.

Guess what, I didn't know anything about the bands playing there, well, you can't know 'em all. MORDRED played only new material, as my buddy told me, but this was counterproductive to the general vibe at the place. Their funky, rapping metalcore had a tough stand among the fans, same went for the other two bands playing there, namely IN THIS LIFE and THE ATOM SEED. You can't have a Sunday every day, simple as it is.

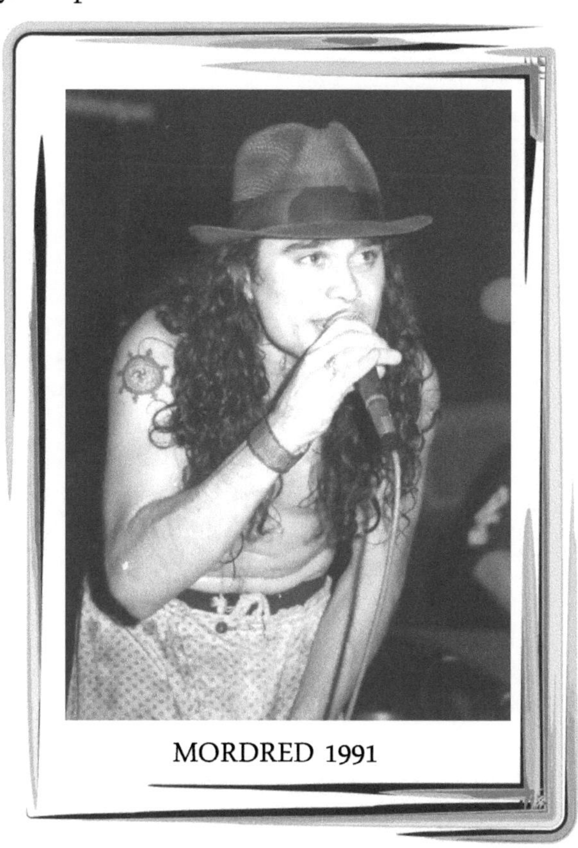

MORDRED 1991

SAVATAGE

To much death on the streets

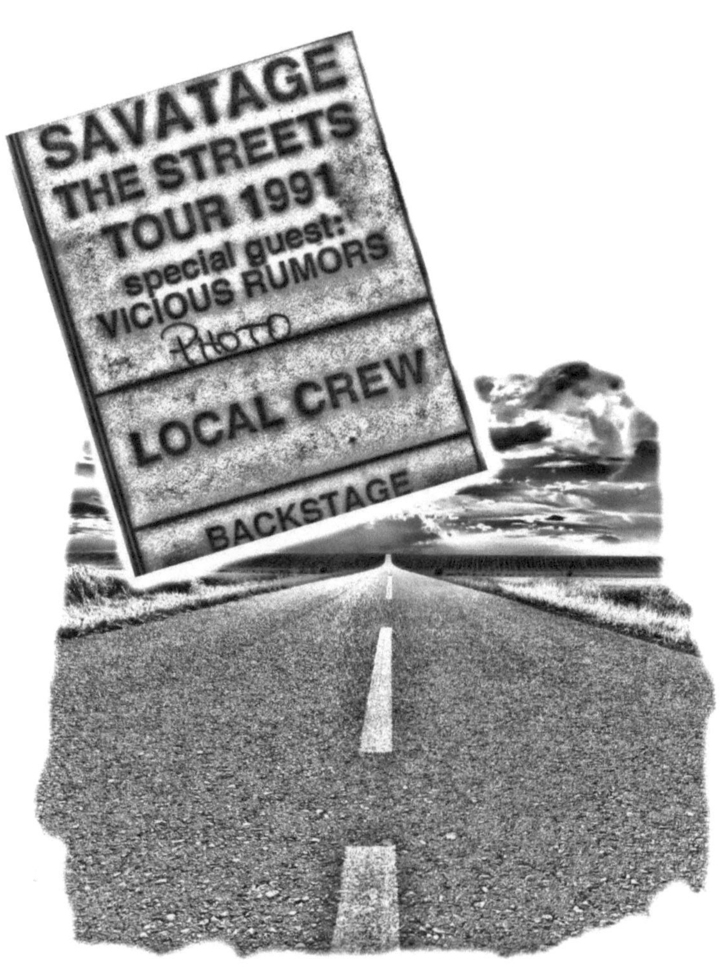

An absolute firework of virtuosity was in store for the fans of SAVATAGE during the" Streets" tour.

Playing at Duesseldorf's TOR3 the support VICIOUS RUMOURS presented themselves in top shape. Definitely one of the most underrated bands out there.

What we didn't know then is that both bands would lose a very important member in the years to follow. Guitarrist Chris Oliva of SAVATAGE being the brother of the vocalist John Oliva died during a heavy car crash 1993 and Carl Albert of VICIOUS RUMOURS had the same incident in 1995 leaving our planet way too soon. Amazing-too much death on the streets.

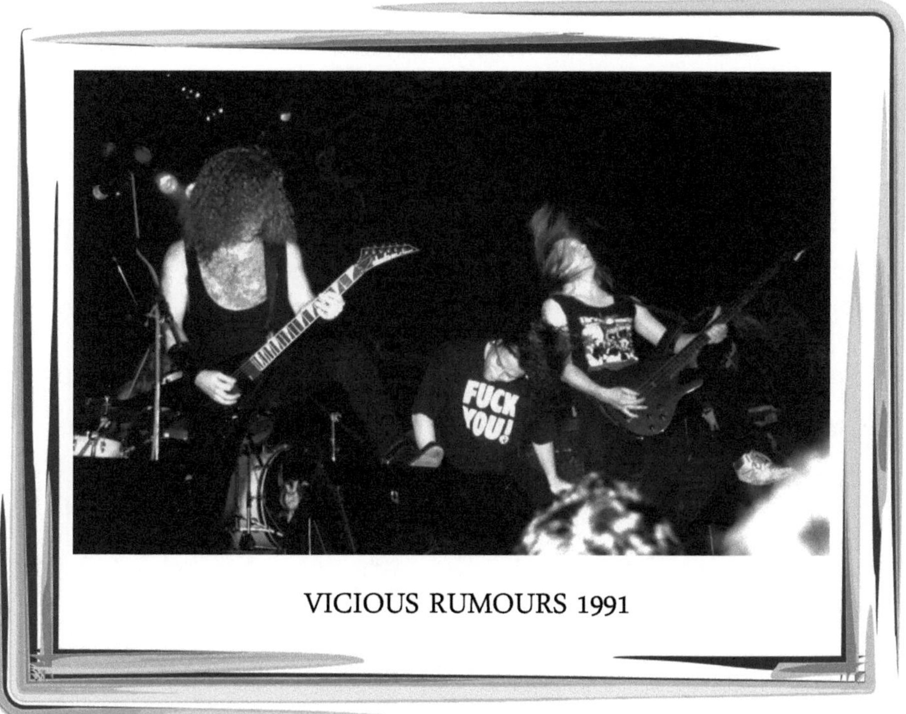

VICIOUS RUMOURS 1991

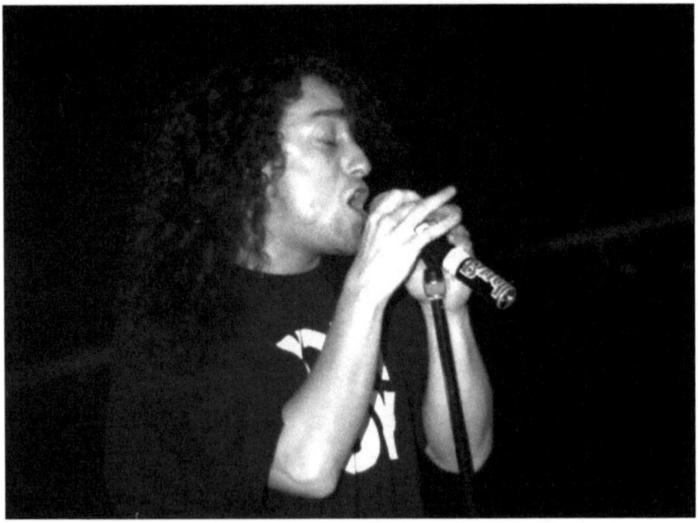

CARL ALBERT (R.I.P.)

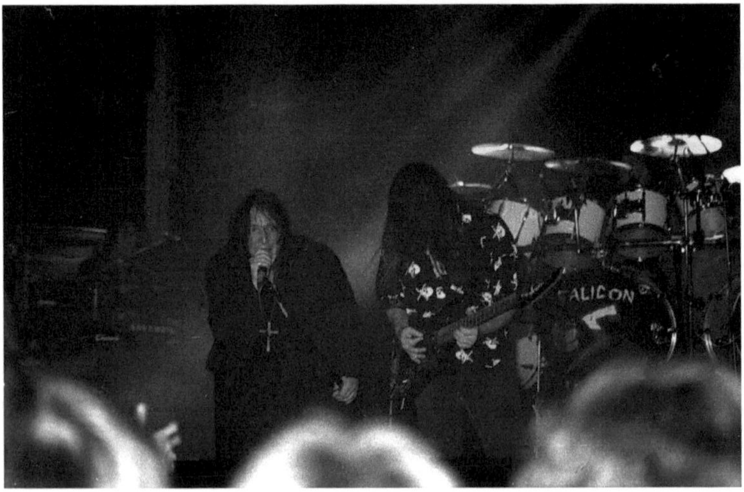

SAVATAGE 1991

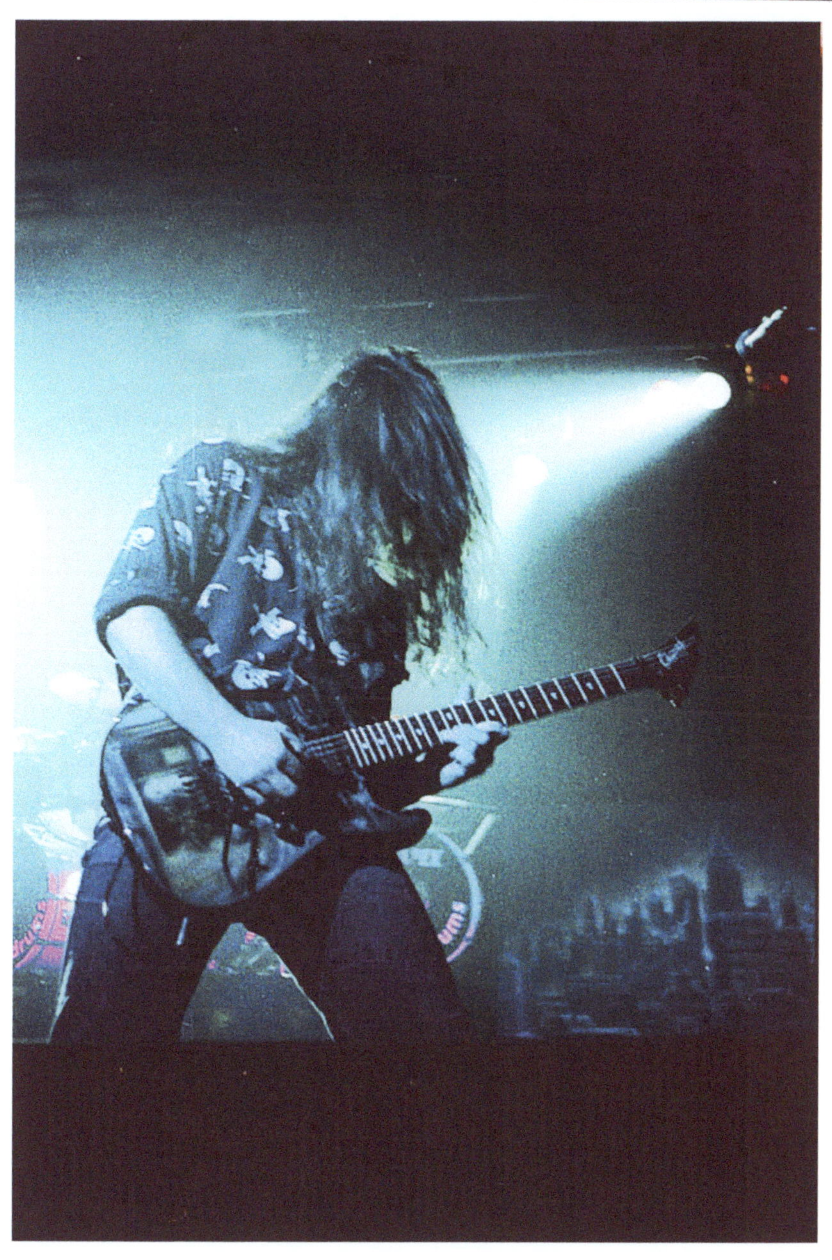

CHRIS OLIVA (R.I.P)

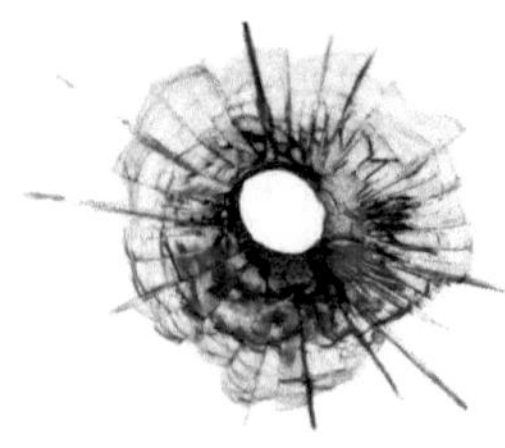

Going broke with backstage passes

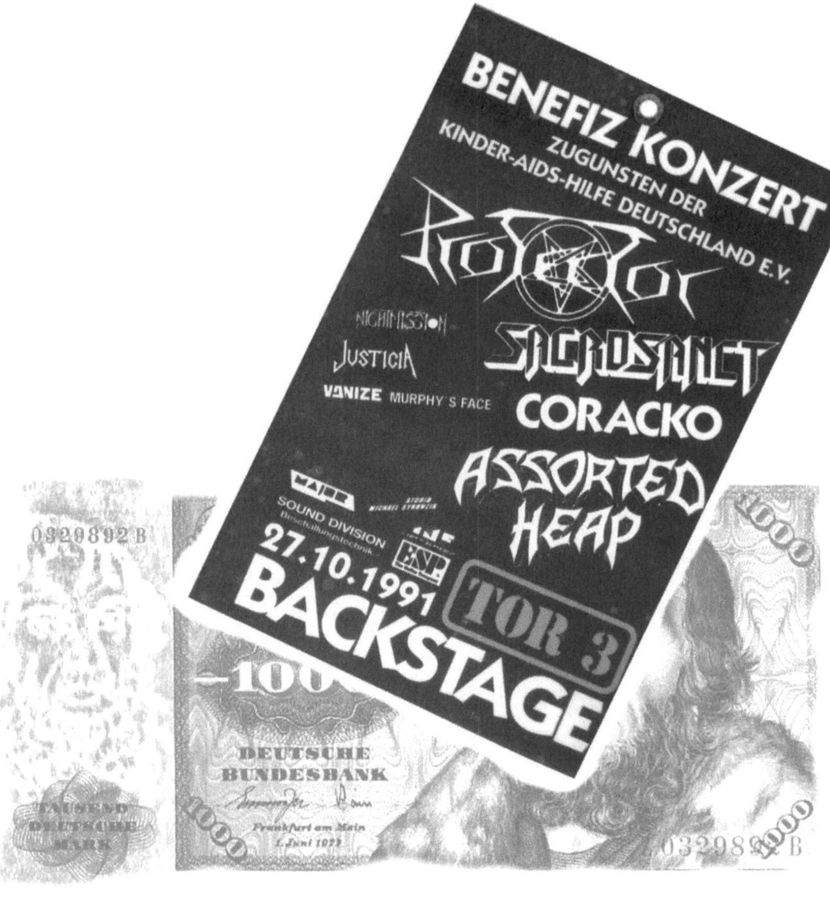

I was pleased when I received the invitation for a beneficiary concert for the kids aids center in Düsseldorf and the had gathered a big line-up of bands: PROTECTOR, SACROCANT, ASSORTED HEAP, CORACKO, NIGHTMISSION, JUSTICIA, VANIZE, MURPHY'S FACE.
I was invited to do a review there.

The only thing that made me skeptical was the low number of attendance when I arrived at TOR3. Is there no interest in the good cause maybe? Or something else went wrong? Maybe because its sunday? Or not enough promotion? The noble gesture of doing something really important for the kids, seemed to be of no interest for the public.

At the end I found at least one reason for this financial holocaust, which was that I saw a vast amount of folks running around with backstage tickets, so these guys didn't bring any money with them. When the whole show was over and it came to paying up for the event, the organizer ended up with a huge debt in his pockets, close to 10k. That's high fee for educational purposes.

I heard that the organizer planned to come back with another event, since he was pissed about the meager outcome and also about his mistakes, which he made.

That's what we also hoped for the kids.

The new Breed

and the power of electricity...

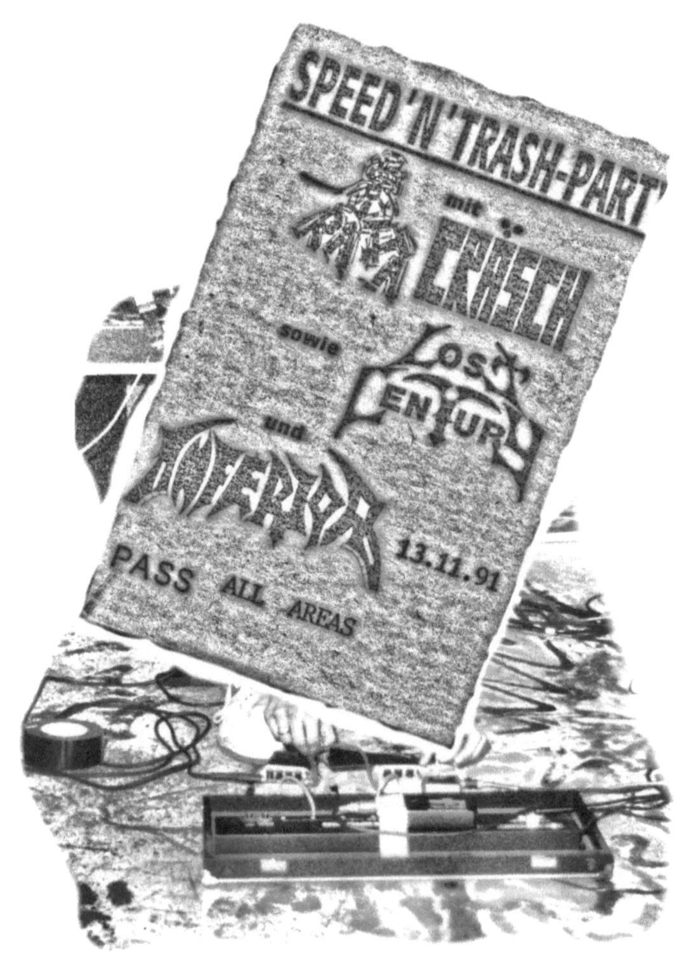

In a fanzine we put focus on and also support regional and up and coming bands. Those gigs happened at way smaller venues than those booked by rockstars.

There was a pub in Wuppertal back then called Kontrast and these guys offered unknown bands the chance to play once a week on Wednesdays.

Event though the day of week is a bad day for gigs, the place was really crowded and the fans and interested guests who wanted to see the three bands INFERIOR, LOST CENTURY, RATTA CRÄSCH, coming from Düsseldorf.

INFERIOR were the opener for the concert reign that evening. They played progressive thrash metal and it was jaw dropping for us spectators to see such high level playing coming from the underground. They didn't play party music, that was for sure, but the audience really appreciated their style.

The next band, playing their first gig ever, were the prog-power—metalheads LOST CENTURY and you could somehow get the impression that they had brought most of the fans to this club. One thing was sure, the level of quality at that night, remained high.

RATTA CRÄSCH were next on the bill and the played a mix of punk and metal which didn't quite make it to the audience that night. At 10:30 pm the enforcers of law came in for a visit and told the organizer that he receives a fair warning now, since the whole concert was way too loud. But the band just kept playing, not giving a shit, well they just got warmed up to say so. It came as it had to come: 20 minutes later somebody cut the power off and that was it for the night, what a bummer!

Everything was so cool that evening, disappointment down to the bone among the fun-metalheads and the fans. After weeks of hard work and planning, sheer joy about the first gig with a new drummer and last but not least the hauling of all the stuff to the place, this end was like a punch in the face for the band.

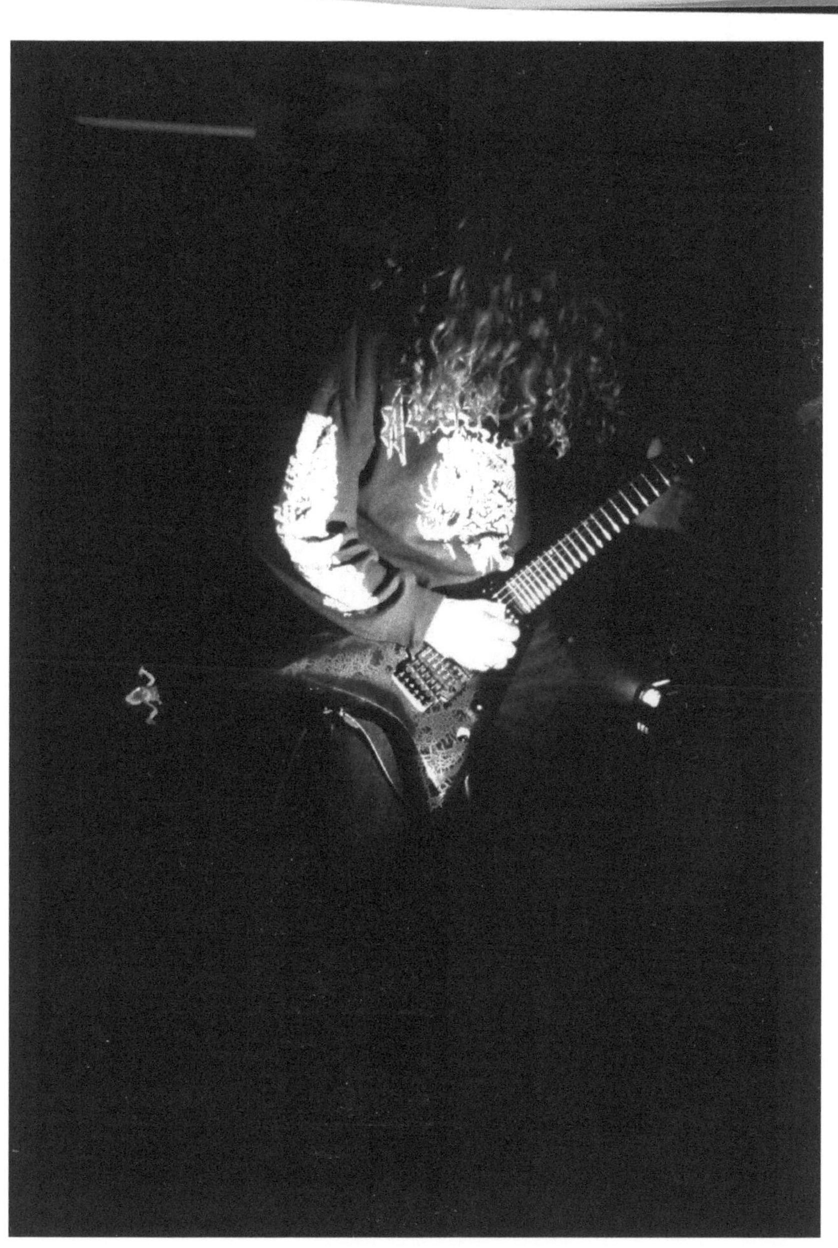

LOST CENTURY 1991

And again...

...year is done...

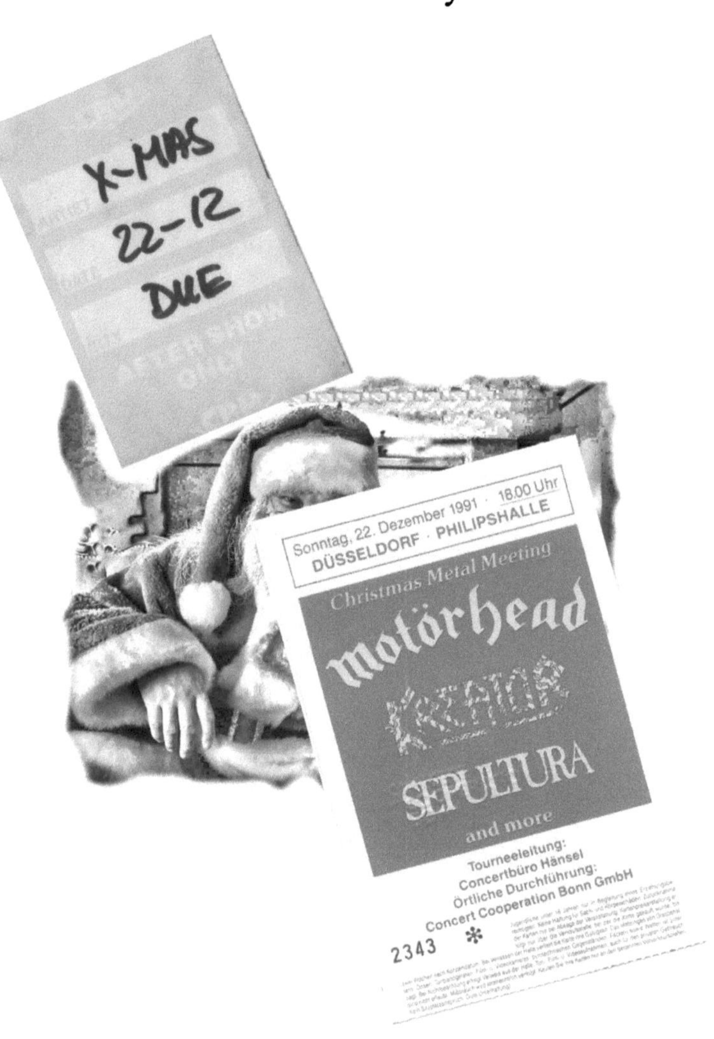

As if it was yesterday (wasn't it yesterday?) LEMMY and friends came by for the annual Christmas bash. The suspicion that they had something like a concert subscription was close.

WOLFSBANE took it easy opening for tonight's show, which was quite a difficult task with all those heavy and aggressive bands on the bill for the show. Two thirds of the 5,000 fans made it outside to the beer booths in the foyer.

The band around Blaize Bayley, who later became the frontman for IRON MAIDEN, left a positive impression though.

All of sudden it got crowded when HEADHUNTER entered the stage. Schmier and his crew presented their first album and spiced things up with a few classics of DESTRUCTION. The happy birthday chorus coming from the audience made this gig a very good one.

MORBID ANGEL had some bad cards, at least with me. I didn't know their material that much and the shitty sound during their performance helped me to give it a rest.

Then the announcer said that Andreas Kisser of SEPULTURA had an accident with his arm, the crowd reacted pretty nervous. SEPULTURA won't play....shit!!!!!!!!!!!!! But then...uno, dos, tres, cuatro: These guys enter the stage with a replacement musician...hats off...intense drumming for sure.

Thinking back about the early days of KREATOR, oh man!

Their sound was always like coming out of a garbage bin, which made you pretty unsure which song they were playing. Today it was a different game, really intense, clear sound and a good lightshow. Thank you guys, awesome!

When Lemmy came, my lights were on and I don't recall any of the show or what has happened, true MOTÖRHEAD style,even journalists need to do that from time to time.

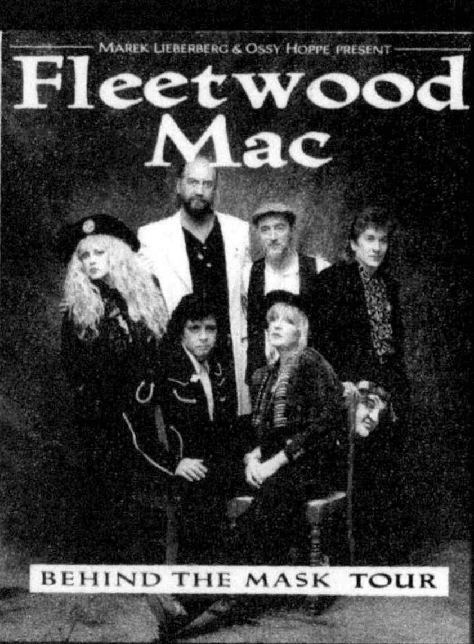

MAREK LIEBERBERG & OSSY HOPPE PRESENT
Fleetwood Mac
BEHIND THE MASK TOUR
7415
Freitag, 7. Sept. 1990 · 20.00 Uhr
ESSEN · GRUGAHALLE
Vorverkauf: DM 42,–
zuzügl. Vorverkaufsgebühr, inkl. 7 % MwSt.
AKKU
LIVE IN DER TAGESZEITUNG
Abendkasse: DM 50,–
inkl. 7 % MwSt.
KEIN SITZPLATZANSPRUCH!
Wichtiger Hinweis siehe Rückseite!

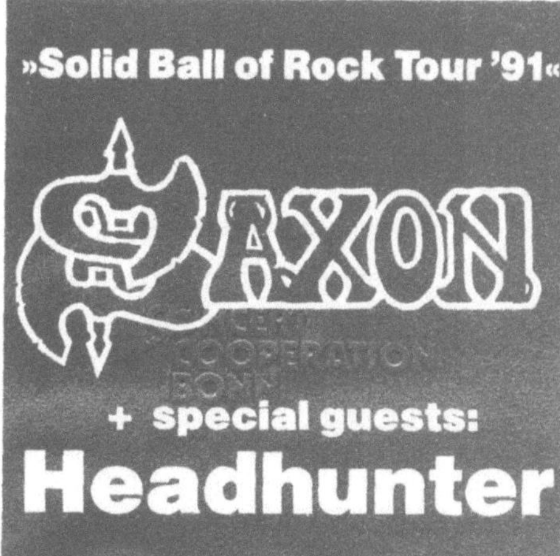

Montag, 13. Mai 1991 · 20.00 Uhr
KÖLN · STADTHALLE MÜLHEIM
»Solid Ball of Rock Tour '91«
SAXON
+ special guests:
Headhunter
Tourneeleitung:
Concertbüro Hänsel
Örtliche Durchführung:
Concert Cooperation Bonn GmbH
1582
Jugendliche unter 18 Jahren nur in Begleitung eines Erziehungsberechtigten. Keine Haftung für Sach- und Körperschäden. Zurücknahme der Karten nur bei Absage der Veranstaltung. Kartenpreiserstattung erfolgt nur über die Verkaufsstelle, bei der die Karte gekauft wurde, bis zwei Wochen nach Konzertdatum. Bei Verlassen der Halle verliert die Karte ihre Gültigkeit. Das Mitbringen von Glasbehältern, Dosen, Tonbandgeräten, Film- u. Videokameras, pyrotechnischen Gegenständen, Fackeln sowie Waffen ist untersagt. Bei Nichtbeachtung erfolgt Verweis aus der Halle. Ton-, Film- u. Videoaufnahmen, auch für den privaten Gebrauch, sind nicht erlaubt. Mißbrauch wird strafrechtlich verfolgt. Kaufen Sie ihre Karten nur an den bekannten Vorverkaufsstellen. Kein Sitzplatzanspruch. Gute Unterhaltung!

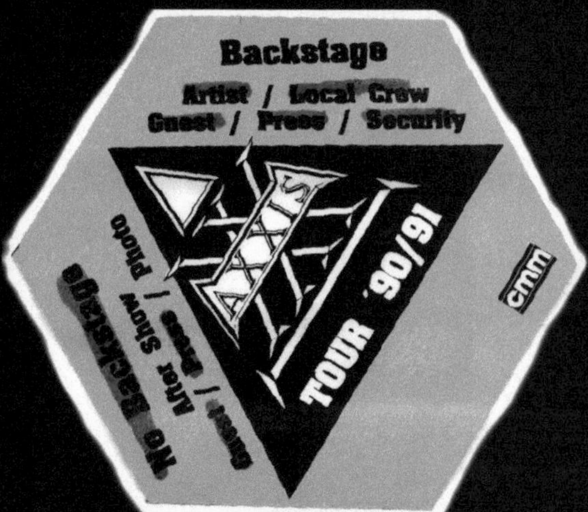

TOURPASS
BRINGS
Colonia 90/91
Kamine Tour '91
GAST
Backstage
Artist / Local Crew
Guest / Press / Security
AXIS
TOUR '90/91
No Backstage
Artist Show / Press
Guest
cnm

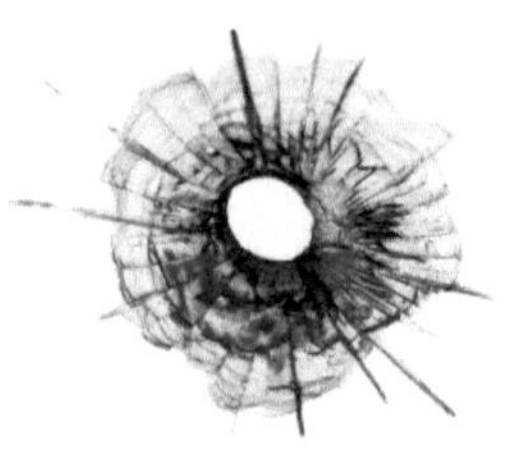

When things got readable he vanished into thin air

During this relatively short time of my paparazzo and reporter existence I experienced quite amusing stories so far. I walked into the time of computers and I witnessed the change of our fanzine cover from black and white to hi-gloss including one extra color.

Even the content was easier to read than in the beginning. We started with 16 pages and after three issues we were double the volume. No, not us but our free fanzine.my time as speeding reporter and paparazzo had just begun and the whole crew was in full bloom.

Only Sascha was different these days...he went more and more out of the spotlight. We all had our opinions but we never ran in arguments, I can say that for sure. Without a final ending we were left alone without our boss and one of us had to continue the task. But who? That's something you will get to know in the second part of this book when it's time again for: "Holli, we have an interview. Guess who it is?"

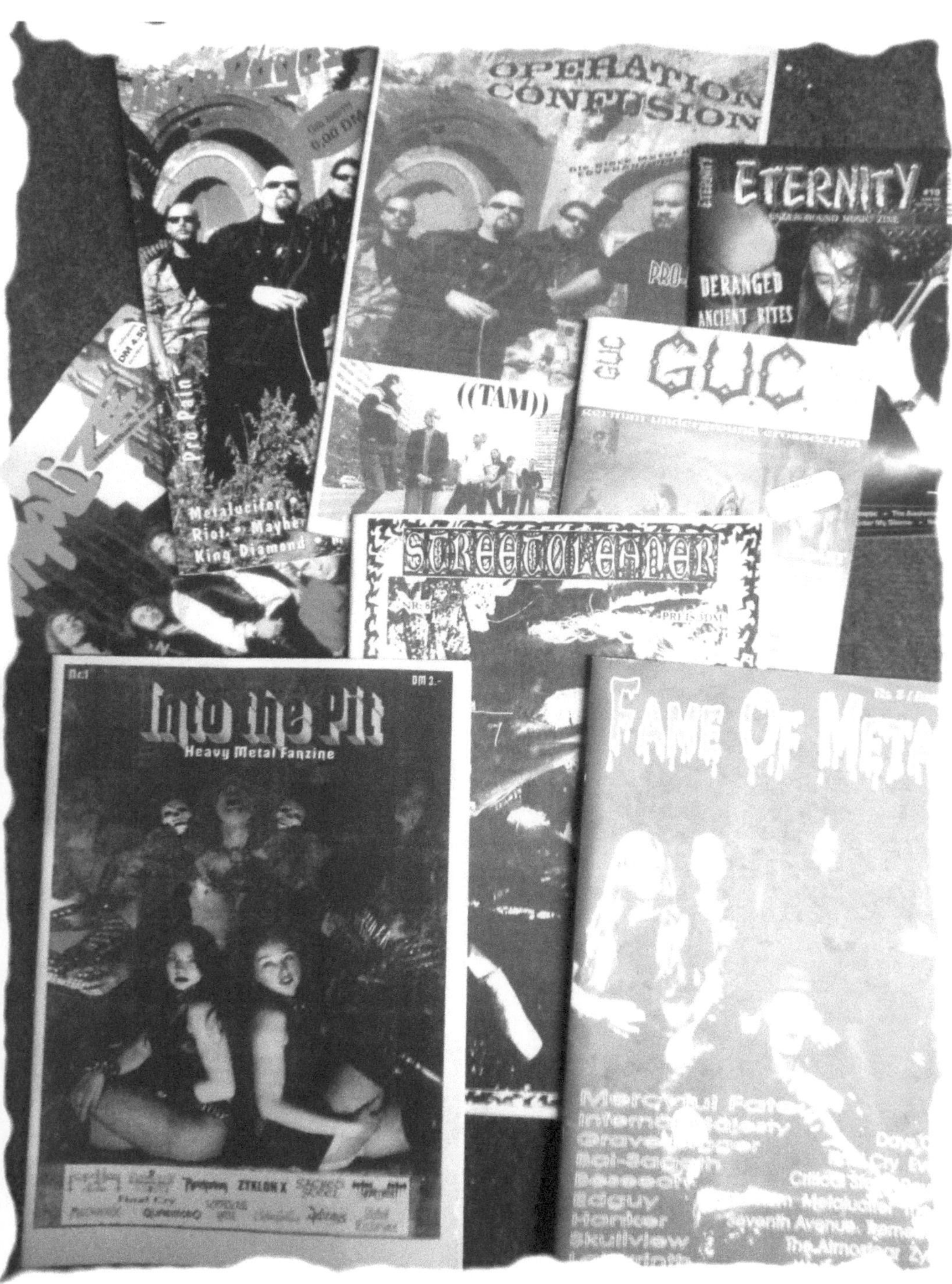
OPERATION CONFUSION
ETERNITY
DERANGED
ANCIENT RITES
G.U.C.
((TAM))
SCREWDRIVER
Pro Pain
Metalucifer
Riot · Mayhem
King Diamond
Into the Pit
Heavy Metal Fanzine
Nr.1
DM 2.-
FAME OF METAL
Mercyful Fate
Gravedigger
Edguy
Skullview

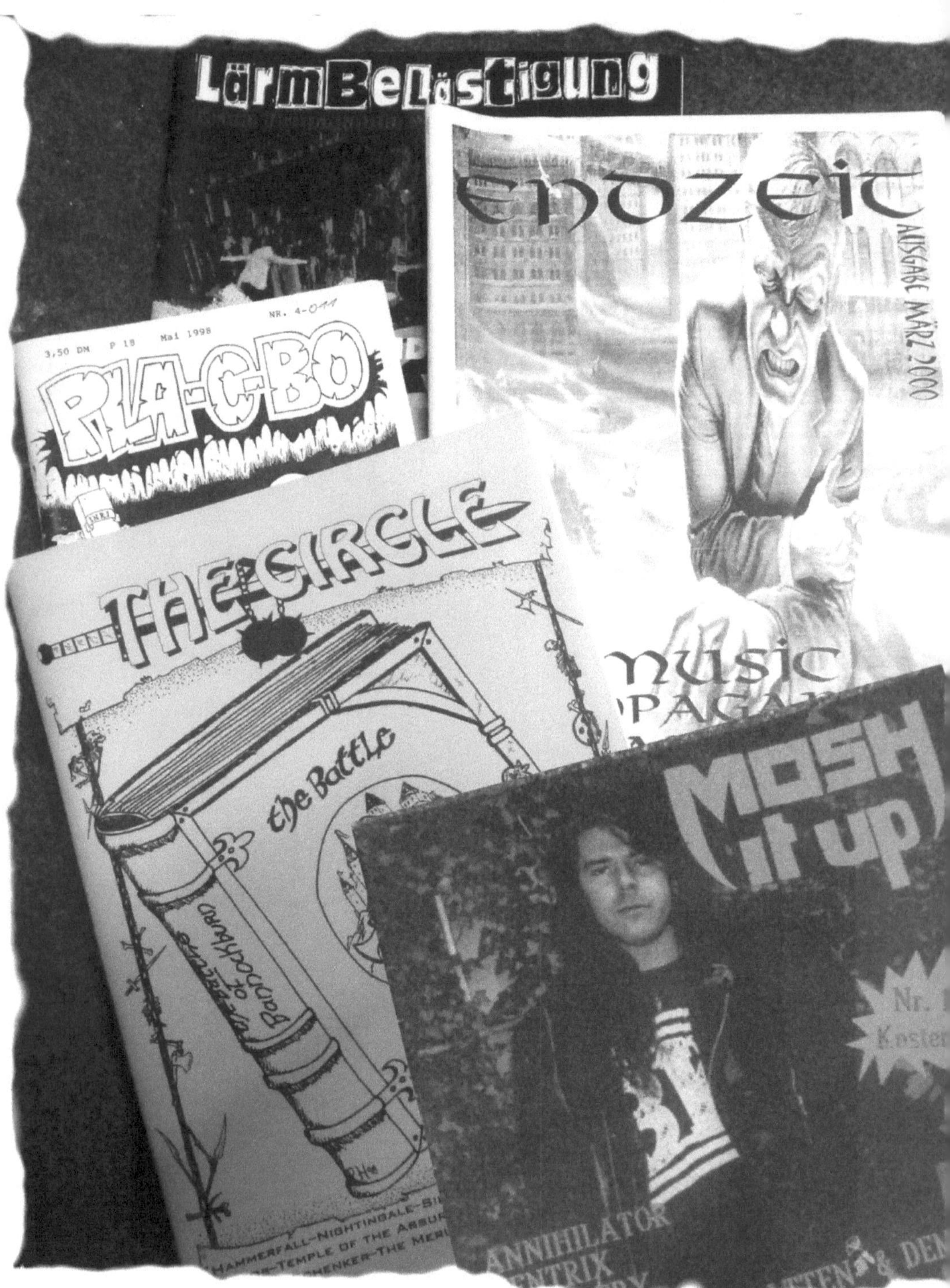
LärmBelästigung
endzeit
AUSGABE MÄRZ 2000
3,50 DM   P 18   Mai 1998
NR. 4-011
PLA-C-BO
THE CIRCLE
the Battle
music
PAGA
MOSH IT UP
Nr.
Kosten
ANNIHILATOR
ENTRIX

So...here it ends for now. I would have loved to offer you all pics in
full color, but that would have increased the costs enormously.
I hope I was a bit entertaining.

Cheers and see you soon.

Holli

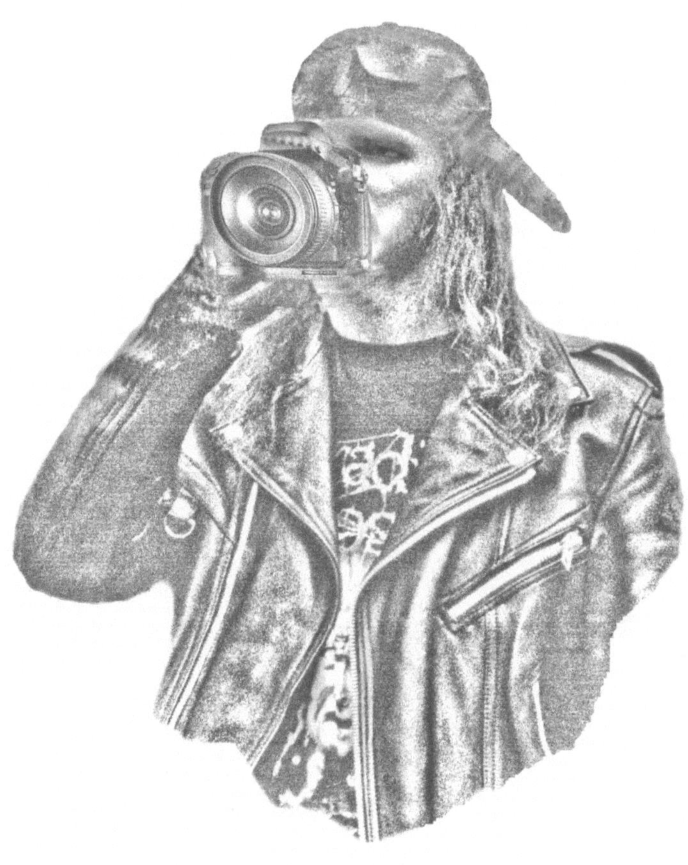